Fromme

MW00399352

THE MOON

A Guide for First-Time Visitors

By Werner "Tiki" Küstenmacher

WITH ILLUSTRATIONS BY THE AUTHOR

TRANSLATED FROM THE GERMAN BY PETER CONSTANTINE

MACMILLAN • USA

Originally published as *Reisen zum Mond,* by Werner "Tiki" Küstenmacher. © 1999 by
Koval Verlag GmbH, 74423 Unterfischach Germany.

Published in the United States by Macmillan Travel
A Pearson Education Macmillan Company
1633 Broadway
New York, NY 10019

Find us online at **www.frommers.com**

ISBN 0-02-862869-1
Library of Congress Number 98-067529

Photographs on pages 27, 53, 59, 60, 68, and 71 from Deutsche Forschungsanstalt für
Luft- und Raumfahrt; photograph on page 43 from *Star Observer* magazine, Vienna.
All other photographs from NASA, the Jet Propulsion Laboratory, the National Space
Science Data Center, and the United States Geological Survey.

Cover photos courtesy of NASA

Printed in Korea

Contents

The Author

Werner "Tiki" Küstenmacher, a German pastor, is a best-selling author and illustrator of over fifty books. He has been fascinated by space travel since early childhood.

This travel guide to the Moon, he tells us, has been the most enjoyable book he has ever worked on— "It's just a pity I had to write about a place I haven't been to yet!"

After writing the book, he feels as if he has been there, and hopes the reader will share this feeling, too. For one thing is certain: Traveling to the Moon is bound to be the deepest spiritual experience of one's life.

Tiki Küstenmacher has made provisions for the future. He already owns a nice plot of land on the Moon. If you want to visit him there, it is near the Gassendi Crater, on the shores of Mare Humorum.

Prelude

The Legend

When Neil Armstrong, the first man on the Moon, climbed back into his lunar lander after his one giant step for mankind, he uttered the enigmatic words: "Good Luck, Mr. Gorsky!"

Many of his coworkers at NASA thought this statement might be a jab directed at a rival astronaut. But no Mr. Gorsky could be found in either the Russian or the American space programs.

For decades, Neil Armstrong's words remained a mystery. But at the beginning of 1997, at a lecture in Tampa Bay, Florida, a reporter resuscitated the twenty-six-year-old question—and Neil Armstrong answered.

It seems that Mr. Gorsky had passed away, and Armstrong felt confident he could safely reveal the truth.

When Neil was a little boy, he and his brother were playing baseball in the garden one day, when one of the balls they hit landed right under the bedroom window of their neighbors—the Gorskys. As Neil climbed the fence to the Gorsky's yard, he heard Mrs. Gorsky shout at her husband: "Oral sex! You want oral sex? You'll get oral sex when the kid next door walks on the Moon!"

The sad thing about this tale is that it is utterly untrue, except for the fact that Neil Armstrong definitely did go to the Moon. And yet this story has been inducted into the Hall of Fame, and with the help of the Internet has spread like wildfire. But as with all legends the question remains: Is there an iota of truth behind it? One can imagine old Sigmund Freud chuckling

down at us from a cloud in the sky. And once again Peter Glaser's theory seems to have been confirmed: Sex is the main driving force behind the popularization of all modern technology (photography, telephone, TV, Internet . . .).

Another slick justification might be that sixty-six-year-old Neil Armstrong sprung this feisty story on the world to jazz up the waning interest in the moon landing.

But the Moon does not need any jazzing up. Today it is as popular as ever. People do their gardening and their cleaning by the Moon; its phases mark the best days for haircuts, making fruit preserves, weeding the garden. Moon, luna, lune, selene—a feminine noun in most languages—has become the leading star of the women's movement, and rules the menstrual cycle, as it does the ebb and flow of the stock market.

More than a quarter of a century has passed since July 20, 1969, when man first stepped on the Moon. Today our romance with the Moon is as passionate as ever. Space travel is now within our reach and is slowly but surely becoming (with or without sex to jazz it up) a popular concept.

The clearest sign of this is that you are reading this book!

The Dream

What a destination! Not too long ago the Moon was thought to be beyond our reach. In 1948 Otto Willi Gail discussed the technical prerequisites of space travel in his acclaimed book *The Physics of Space Travel*. In this book we find the words: "We will not even broach the problem of landing on another celestial body. That possibility lies too far in the future." It was only twenty-one years later that *Apollo 11* landed on the Moon.

Space travel is controversial. It is as insane a dream as the dream of flying or the dream of sailing across the seas. There are many obstacles, ranging from the ecological to the economic, from the incredible danger involved to the health risks of man in space. And yet man is never hampered by cool logic in his unstoppable quest to overcome all barriers.

To date, twelve people have traveled to the Moon, and many hundreds have circled Earth in space. Each and every one of them was moved by the experience, coming back to Earth a different person. They set out fuelled by scientific curiosity, thirst for adventure, and fascination with technology. But when they returned, they spoke mainly of their transcendental, spiritual experience in the vast distance from Earth. And we begin to suspect how many fetters keep us within the boundaries of our planet and what an undreamt-of wealth might lie in the possibility of freeing oneself—at least for a short while—from these fetters.

Why Now?

The science writer Hagen Thorgesson points out that there was a 280-year lapse between the invention of the steam engine, which set off the Industrial Revolution, and man's first step on the Moon.

In Roman times, Hero of Alexandria invented a prototype of the steam engine, but the Romans didn't bother developing it. If they had, by A.D. 800 at the latest, Charlemagne would have been sending his generals to the Moon. When you measure what mankind has achieved against what mankind *could* have achieved, the results are really disappointing, Thorgesson concludes.

In Roman times man was not interested in space. The large number of slaves meant that there was no need for inventing machines to make life easier. Technological progress only begins when many people want it over a long period of time. A clear sign that this was happening was the increasing number of novels about moon travel written since 1700.

The final technological thrust came with World War II. Hitler dreamed of a secret weapon that would give Germany international supremacy. Wernher von Braun's development of the relatively light-weight V2 rocket cost approximately

> "I always keep telling myself that tomorrow will be beautiful, and that all my dreams will come true. If you believe you can fly to the Moon, then you will fly there."
> *Sophia Loren*

$2 billion. As there were no computers, and it was not possible to accurately measure distances in space, German scientists had to rely on trial and error, and there were hundreds of quite spectacular misfires before they finally got a handle on the rocket principle.

Twenty years later, the development of *Saturn V* (again under the supervision of the same Wernher von Braun) cost the equivalent of a small V2 rocket. With the technological advances in engineering, only two launch tests were needed for the gigantic and highly complex machine to be declared safe for transporting manned capsules to the Moon.

This time it was the Cold War that gave space travel its decisive thrust. On April 12, 1961, Soviet astronaut Yuri Gagarin was the first man in space, a propaganda coup that Soviet Premier Nikita Krushchev utilized to the fullest. Within six weeks President Kennedy, in a desperate attempt to salvage the United States' international image, declared that by the end of the decade America would land a man on the Moon "and return him safely back to Earth."

It was this national objective, supported by the American people, that fuelled the accelerated development that made President Kennedy's promise come true on July 20, 1969.

Why Not Mars?

After *Pathfinder*'s spectacular Mars landing on July 6, 1997, the dream of sending a manned rocket to the red planet once again became popular. If we are setting our sights on space travel, why not Mars?

There are many reasons that argue against tourism on Mars. Whenever man ventures into new territory, he first explores it, and colonization follows only much later. In the case of the Moon, colonization could well start in the next ten to twenty years. But in the case of Mars, a planet still relatively unexplored, this will take much longer.

You can't fly straight to Mars. To get there, you would first have to orbit the Sun in a gigantic elliptical curve in order to build up the momentum you need. As a result,

Show-off!

there are only specific times during the year when Mars missions can be launched. The length of the flight and the duration of the stay are determined by the position of Earth in relation to Mars. If the two planets are in opposition, then the flight lasts 254 days, the stay 20, and the flight back another 254. If the two planets are in conjunction, the flight takes 27 days, but the mandatory stay there would be 530 days, and the flight back, 209.

One thing is clear: Mars will not become a major tourist destination anytime soon. You could never get that kind of time off from work. Traveling to the red planet is a major undertaking for which you'd need to set aside at least three years. And then there is the limited entertainment value of such a trip. The lion's share of the trip is across open space, with no spectacular vistas of planets or other heavenly bodies, and Mars itself does not offer the incredible view of Earth that the Moon does. Compared to Mars, the Moon is not only closer to home, but also far more attractive.

A Short History of the Moon

The origin of the Moon remained shrouded in mystery for many years, and even after astronauts and lunar probes were sent up to take a closer look, many questions have remained unanswered. This is how we now think it all started:

A Cosmic Catastrophe

It all happened about 4.6 billion years ago. Earth was very young, a fiery yellow ball of molten lava, rotating much faster than it does today—one rotation took only four hours and forty minutes.

Back then, cosmic balls of fire still rained down on the hot, bubbling Earth, and a celestial body the size of a small planet crashed into it, hurling large chunks of fiery material into space. Following the laws of physics, these chunks orbited Earth for a long time, gradually coalescing into our Moon.

Even if Earth and the Moon look very different today, geologically speaking they are sisters.

Heading for the goal

Oceans of Stone

The energy from countless collisions of fragments made the Moon's outer layer melt hundreds of kilometers deep. The heavier elements sank, and it was only after some 200 million years that the outer crust began to harden again.

With the passage of time, the Earth-Moon system gradually began losing force. Earth's rotation slowed down and the Moon moved away.

Initially, the Moon circled Earth at a distance of 35,600 kilometers (22,072 miles)—today it is more than ten times that. A trend that has kept up: Every year the Moon moves 3.48 centimeters (1.36 inches) farther away. That is the price it pays for the energy it loses by making the tides rise and fall.

In the meantime, the bombardment of the Moon from the solar system continued, leaving myriad craters of all sizes on its surface. For a long time the area beneath the skin of the Moon remained liquid, and the larger craters filled with molten lava creating smooth areas.

In the past, these flat plains were thought to be oceans, and to this day they are still called that. And the term is not completely wrong because the plains were once covered with liquid rock, which, as it cooled, created impressive ravines, chasms, and canyons. Three billion years ago the inner activity of the Moon ceased, as did the bombardment of its surface, which is not protected by an atmosphere. A thick layer of up to 20 meters (66 feet) of dust and loose dirt covered the surface.

The Moon

Surface: 37,960,000 km^2 (1,480,440 sq. mi.); 7.4% of Earth's surface

Diameter: 3,476 km (2,155 mi.)

Equatorial circumference: 10,920 km (6,770 mi.)

Volume: 21,990,000 km^3 (5,240,832.72 cu. mi.); 2% of Earth's volume

Mass: 73.5 trillion tons; 1.2% of Earth's mass

Mean density: 60% of Earth's density

Shortest distance from Earth (Perigee): 356,400 km (220,968 mi.)

Farthest distance from Earth (Apogee): 406,700 km (252,154 mi.)

Mean distance from Earth: 384,401 km (238,329 mi.); approximately 30 times the Earth's diameter

Time needed for light to reach Earth: 1.3 seconds

Temperature on the dark side: −170°C to −185°C (−274°F to −301°F)

Temperature on the light side: +130°C (266°F)

Constant temperature at 1 meter (3.3 feet) depth: −35°C (−95°F)

Brightness of the full Moon: 0.25 Lux

Brightness of full Earth: As seen from the Moon, 16 Lux

Number of inhabitants: 0

Number of visitors: 12 (all white American males)

Single large meteor impacts formed craters marked by bright

aureoles of disgorged material. One of the youngest of these craters is Tycho, which is thought to be about 100 million years old.

The Last of the Moon Volcanoes

There was a meteor impact witnessed by man. On June 25, 1178, five English monks saw "a flaming torch spat hot coals and sparks over a considerable distance."

And in fact the young crater, Giordano Bruno, lies right on the edge of the visible side of the Moon where the monks reported seeing flames.

The Apollo program came up with indirect proof that the eight-hundred-year-old sighting was real. The astronauts left a mirror on the Moon to enable precise laser measurements of the Moon's distance from Earth. And sure enough, every three years, the Moon swings about 3 meters (9.9 feet) back and forth—precisely the effect that an impact eight hundred years ago would have caused.

Craters Galore

From the time man began studying the Moon with a telescope, he also began speculating on the origin of the countless rings of mountains on its surface. Were they extinct volcanoes or cones formed by meteor impacts? It wasn't until the first space probes sent back their data that it became clear that almost all the craters on the Moon were the result of impacts from outer space. Only a few craters could be the result of volcanic eruptions.

The number of moon craters confirms our estimates of the number of meteorites that hurtled through our solar system throughout the ages. For the first billion or so years of their existence, Earth and the Moon were constantly bombarded from outer space. On our planet hardly any evidence of this barrage remains. But on the Moon, where there are no atmospheric conditions or shifting landmasses to eradicate the traces, all the craters have survived.

Lunar Landscapes on Earth

One of the largest surviving meteor craters on Earth is the Popigai Crater north of Krasnoyarsk in central Russia. More than forty million years ago a meteor measuring several kilometers in diameter must have impacted there. The imprint it left is 100 kilometers (62 miles) in diameter and up to 250 meters (825 feet) deep. The collision sent shock waves over Earth that were fifty times stronger than the most powerful volcanic eruption.

There have also been a number of cataclysmic impacts in the United States, the largest of which came thirty-five million years ago and left a crater hidden beneath the Chesapeake Bay twice the size of Rhode Island and nearly as deep as the Grand Canyon. It was the most dramatic ecological disaster ever to hit the eastern United States. At impact there were lethal flashes of light and heat shocks measuring tens of thousands of degrees Celsius. Gigantic gas streams sent melting rock and debris hurtling into the stratosphere. All life within

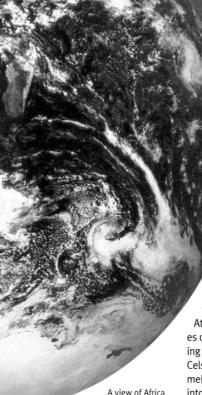

A view of Africa

Giambattista Riccoli also picked up on his colleague Lanterns' idea of naming moon craters after astronomers and famous people, and bestowed two hundred names in chronological sequence from north to south. In the nineteenth century, the German astronomers Schröter and Mädler refined this nomenclature, adding 427 new entries, including names of smaller craters (printed in Latin uppercase letters) and elevations (printed in Greek lowercase letters).

In the following decades there was such pandemonium in the naming of the Moon landscape that in 1935 the International

a radius of hundreds of miles was destroyed.

Charting the Moon

Giambattista Riccoli, a Jesuit from Bologna, drew up the first serviceable map of the Moon in 1651. Following the example of the German astronomer Hevelius, Riccoli called the Moon's dark surfaces *maria,* "oceans" or "seas." The common belief was that the Moon influenced the weather on Earth. The principle was simple: The waxing Moon brought good weather, the waning Moon, bad.

As a result, the *maria* in the first quarter of the Moon were given names such as "Sea of Tranquility" and "Sea of Serenity," whereas the *maria* in the final quarter of the waning Moon still have names like "Ocean of Storms" and "Sea of Showers."

Meteorite Danger for Moon Tourists
Nowadays there is not much danger of a moon tourist being struck by a meteorite. About one 2-pound meteorite strikes every 200 square kilometers (124 square miles) of the Moon every month. The risk of being hit by one of these meteorites is no greater than being struck by lightning on Earth.

Rock samples brought back by the Apollo missions also show traces of micrometeorites that are only visible under a microscope, but their frequency of impact has largely diminished in our era. The risk of meteorite impacts, however, will have to be taken into account when long-term building projects are initiated on the Moon.

Astronomical Union (I.A.U.) finally commissioned Blagg and Müller to standardize the 681 names that had been coined up to that time.

Nowadays only scientists of exceptional merit have a moon crater named after them.

The Dispute over Crater Names

After the photographing of the far side of the Moon in 1959, and the moon landing in 1969, in 1970 the I.A.U. accepted 513 new names for moon formations, particularly on the far side. Since the first pictures of the far side came from Soviet probes, these names are predominantly of Russian scientists. Also for the first time, living people were to be immortalized on the Moon—six American astronauts and six Soviet cosmonauts.

In 1973 a controversy arose concerning the use of Latin and Greek letters (Kepler C, for instance, is a smaller crater near the Kepler Crater), and the decision was reached to gradually begin giving the smaller craters their own names. This decision was partially reversed again in 1976, with the result that many smaller moon formations now have two names. To date there are 6,231 named craters on the side of the Moon facing Earth, 801 of which have their own names. The remaining moon formations have Latin names by which you can orient yourselves as you plan your moon trip.

Moon Latin	
Catena	crater chain
Dorsa	a system of ocean ridges
Dorsum	an ocean ridge
Lacus	lake
Mare	sea
Maria	seas
Mons	mountain
Montes	mountains
Oceanus	ocean
Palus	marsh
Promontorium	cape
Rima	channel
Rimae	channels
Rupes	fissure or crevice
Sinus	bay
Vallis	valley

Getting Your Bearings

The magnetic field on the Moon is barely measurable. As a result, a compass will not be of much help as you trek through the rough lunar terrain.

Consequently, before the first steps are taken to begin building settlements on the Moon, a satellite system will have to be set up. Since the Moon has no atmosphere, conventional radio communication is limited to the range of visibility—which is not very far, as the lunar horizon is already noticeable at 2.5 kilometers (1.55 miles).

A lunar positioning system (LPS) will be installed in these satellites and will provide moon tourists with quick and easy orientation on their exploratory trips.

The Moon— From a Terrestrial Perspective

The Moon rotates once on its axis every time it orbits Earth—therefore the same side always faces us, a phenomenon linked with our oceans' tidal flows.

The Moon's gravity causes two bulges on Earth's body of water: a tidal bulge facing the Moon, and another facing the opposite side of the globe. Because our planet rotates, these bulges shift over the Earth's surface, causing the rising and falling of the tides. The Moon also causes solid ground to rise and fall imperceptibly.

Because these tidal and terrestrial bulges shift in the direction opposite to that in which Earth is turning, the Moon is gradually slowing Earth's rotation. In the not-too-distant past, days were noticeably shorter. And a few thousand years from now, many an executive's dream will finally come true: twenty-five-hour days will be a reality.

Earth as a Brake

Earth also has a tidal effect on the Moon, and a markedly stronger

one at that—after all, Earth's mass is eighty-one times that of the Moon. Our strong-armed planet managed to curb the Moon's rotation relatively quickly, until it stopped completely in relation to Earth. Our Moon (probably like many other moons) is firmly "latched"

into an unyielding orbital speed in relation to Earth.

Libration

Those of you wishing to view your future flight destination from a terrestrial perspective will not be able to dodge this technical term. The Moon does not circle Earth in a precise orbital plane, but at a slight ellipse. As a result, its speed changes during its orbit: when the Moon is nearest Earth, it travels at its highest speed (its own rotation, however, always stays the same). From the point when the Moon is closest to Earth, it travels a quarter of its orbital plane in less time than it takes for it to rotate 90 degrees on its axis. As a result, we see the Moon inclining slightly to the left during this period and we get to peek over the right edge of its hemisphere. The exact opposite happens on its return journey.

Added to this "libration in length" there is also a "libration in breadth." The Moon's axis of rotation is inclined at 6.7 degrees to Earth's orbital plane, as a result of which the Moon alternately inclines its north and its south poles toward Earth. These inclinations in length and breadth occur simultaneously and keep bringing different parts of the Moon's surface into view. The lunar areas intermittently in sight are known as *libration zones*. This is why we are able to observe 59 percent of the Moon from Earth instead of only 50 percent.

Even Binoculars Will Do the Trick

For a basic look at the Moon, binoculars will do the trick. Note the number combination on the binoculars before you buy them: The first number signifies the magnification, the second the diameter of the outer lens in millimeters.

For instance, 8×50 binoculars will magnify an object eight times, and a 50-millimeter lens is the minimum requirement for a nighttime viewing of the sky.

The most important accessory, however, is a tripod. At these relatively low magnifications the binoculars must be held absolutely still for details of the Moon's surface to be visible.

Buying a Telescope

Acquiring a telescope is even better. Here, too, a tripod is almost more important than the lens. A 100× or 200× magnification might sound great, but it says little about the telescope's quality. A better standard is the light-gathering diameter of the objective. It is measured in inches, and its size has a marked effect on its price.

A 3-inch objective is good enough for basic moon viewing. Whether you opt for a classic lens telescope or a mirror telescope is a question of taste. A mirror telescope is short, fat, easy to carry, and simple to manufacture. The longer lens telescope will give you a better quality picture and will also make a bigger impression on the neighbors.

Even with a telescope of 50× magnification you will notice Earth's rotation as the stars shift relatively quickly out of your field of vision. To remedy this you can acquire a tripod with a (costly) parallax device, which has an axis aligned to the Earth's axis with which you can keep the equipment "adjusted."

Interestingly enough, the best view of your travel destination is not necessarily during a full Moon. The contrasts of the lunar landscape are at their most impressive and the surface features most distinct when the sunlight is reflected at an angle.

The Himalayas

Space-Travel Basics

One of the earliest theoretical problems in space travel was the speed needed to escape Earth's gravity.

The Speed Question

To reach an orbital plane one needs a speed of 7.9 kilometers per minute (4.9 miles per minute), a whopping 28,440 kilometers per hour (17,632.8 miles per hour). In his novel *From the Earth to the Moon*, Jules Verne has a projectile shot out of a gigantic cannon. Not a good idea. The highest speed at which a terrestrial cannon could shoot a projectile would be about 4,000 kilometers per hour (2,480 miles per hour). Even if this cannon could generate ten times that velocity and still withstand the immense temperatures it would generate, the projectile would burn up in the intense resistance of the atmosphere.

Another important question is the maximum pressure the human body can stand. We do not actually sense speed. We endure the 108,000 kilometers per hour (66,960 miles per hour) with which our Earth races around the Sun

without the slightest problem. What *is* dangerous for us, however, are abrupt changes in speed. If Earth were to speed up or slow down by just 1 percent, all life would abruptly come to an end.

Jules Verne's space travelers would have been crushed to a pulp by the pressure of extreme acceleration within the first seconds after being fired out of the cannon — in other words, they wouldn't have even survived the takeoff.

A healthy human being can easily submit to an increase of speed of up to 25 meters per second (82.5 feet per second). The resulting pressure corresponds to two times that of a person's weight (2.5 g = $2^1/_2$ times the normal acceleration in a free fall, which is approximately 10 meters per second (33 feet per second). Accordingly, the necessary speed could be reached within eight minutes at a distance of 2,500 kilometers (1,550 miles).

In reality it takes a little longer because air resistance acts as a brake. But the momentum of the

Old-fashioned flying machine: a Gemini rocket

Earth's rotation can be used effectively during liftoff. This is why your trip to the Moon will most probably begin at a location near the equator, because that's where Earth's rotatory momentum is at its most powerful.

New Scientific Discoveries

The most important part of any plan to one day colonize the Moon will be the search for water. For many years, scientists believed that there could be no reservoirs of liquid on the Moon. Billions of years of intensive solar radiation and the absence of any kind of atmosphere would have dried up any water.

A Sensational Find

Early in 1998, the American *Lunar Prospector* satellite found the first signs that indicated there might well be water at the Moon's poles. It seems that there are craters at the North Pole and areas in the Aitken Basin at the South Pole where the Sun's rays never reach. Blocks of meteorite ice seem to have survived.

The *Lunar Prospector*'s highly sensitive neutron spectrometer indicated that there might be water supplies ranging from ten

"Go figure! When a guy has a good idea, it gets snatched up right away!"

million to three hundred million tons, but spread over an area of 50,000 square kilometers (19,500 square miles).

The spectrometer can locate water that lies up to half a meter beneath the surface.

There will be more specific data available when the *Lunar Prospector* flies as close as 10 kilometers (6.2 miles) over the Moon's surface in 1999.

Lunar Colonies

A rich supply of water would be the single most important factor for manufacturing oxygen and cultivating plants. One could even turn the water into rocket fuel with the help of the limitless supply of solar energy. As the American astronomer Eugene Shoemaker put it, finding water on the Moon would turn it into the solar system's second most valuable piece of real estate. The astronaut Philip Chapman calculated that the water supplies on the Moon represent a net value of $9 trillion.

But not everyone agrees on the feasibility of putting the Moon's water to use. John Lewis of Tucson University has pointed out that there are some overwhelming problems, such as transporting water from the poles. According to him, water is a secondary resource on the Moon.

Catastrophes

Space travel is a risky endeavor, sometimes with fatal results. The three astronauts of *Apollo 1* (1967) perished in a cabin fire during a test, and the crew of *Soyuz 1* (1967) and *Soyuz 11* (1971) lost their lives during touchdown.

The failed start of *Apollo 13* ("Houston, we have a problem"), which luckily did have a happy ending, even made it to the big screen.

The greatest catastrophe came in 1986 with the explosion of the space shuttle *Challenger*, seventy-three seconds after liftoff. Seven astronauts lost their lives.

Moon Tourism

It wasn't long after the first Moon landing in July of 1969 that it became clear that the United States was not going to be able to keep up its breakneck tempo in the space race.

Not that there was a lack of national enthusiasm. America was in the grip of an unprecedented space fever—expensive museums were set up, a flight to Mars was planned.

But the money ran out. The Apollo program had cost $24 billion (this is the amount most often quoted), and in 1965, during the height of the space race, almost 1 percent of the United States' gross national product was spent on the space program. This could not be kept up on a long-term basis.

Tourism and Money

Today the American space program has been turned into a hard-nosed commercial enterprise. But the massive investments in the space shuttle have brought a good return. The United States is the unrivaled provider of this high-end service, and there is no lack of clients. Satellites now play a key role in many fields of research, as do manned experiments in space.

Beginning to build the large International Space Station, the ISS, is a vital step toward lunar tourism. On December 10, 1998, the Russian *Zarya Module* laid the foundation stone in space. In the following forty-five scheduled shuttle flights, over one hundred parts of the space station will be taken into

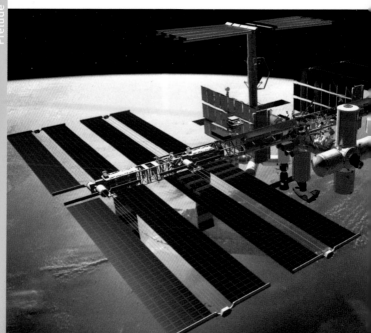

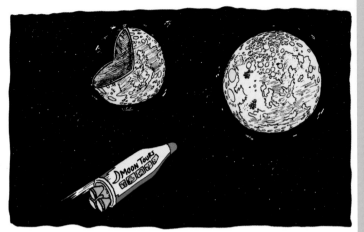

"Business is so good, they've had to expand."

orbit and connected up—all in all, 460 tons of the most valuable high-tech material we have.

The $20 billion space station, measuring 80 meters (264 feet) long by 108 meters (356.4 feet) wide, will be ready in 2004. It will orbit Earth at a height of 407 kilometers (252.34 miles) at a speed of 29,000 kilometers per hour (17,980 miles per hour). There will always be seven astronauts living on the station. It is only with a space-station stopover that the first plans for a moon base can be drawn up.

That such a moon base will be of momentous scientific importance is uncontestable. But when it comes to the financial side, tourism will play a vital role.

Rich Eccentrics First

This guidebook will give you a clear appraisal of your chances of ever visiting the Moon as a tourist. This will be the scenario: The moment a moon base is set up, tourism will begin—because it is a perfect opportunity for economic gain.

The first tourists will be journalists paid for by a TV station or a

The International Space Station

> "There is a clarity, a brilliance to space that simply doesn't exist on Earth, even on a cloudless summer's day in the Rockies, and nowhere else can you realize so fully the majesty of our Earth and be so awed at the thought that it's only one of untold thousands of planets."
>
> *Gus Grissom* (Mercury 4, Gemini 3)

media conglomerate. Or enormously rich adventurers and eccentrics.

The next moon tourists might well be winners of a media-blitz lottery. But then it will be the turn of the average travel buff wishing to make a cherished dream come true: Someone like you.

Stumbling Blocks

It is vital that catastrophes be avoided on the way to the Moon. Space travel is still a highly complex endeavor filled with unforeseeable risks. Space debris hurtling around Earth poses a real threat, as does the danger of a powerful meteor impact, the astronaut's worst nightmare since space travel began. Not to mention the countless little glitches that time and again have led to disaster. Imagine a disaster in which paying customers lose their lives instead of hardened test pilots and veteran scientists! For the first time the world would really start questioning the viability of space travel. For this reason alone, space tourism will begin only once the pioneer phase is over and space flights have become routine, just as the shuttle flights have.

The Price

The price for a shuttle liftoff ranges between $50 million and $250 million—depending on whether the satellites being transported are included or not. A shuttle could hold a cabin with a seating capacity of up to forty passengers, which would still come to more than a million dollars per person.

At a later stage, when ground personnel are reduced and newer technology is in place, a simple shuttle flight orbiting Earth a couple of times is estimated to cost around $50,000, a stay in the space station about twice that amount.

But reliable price estimates for traveling to the Moon are still a thing of the future. Only when the basic infrastructure—a space station, a lunar orbital station, and a moon base—are up and running, will we be able to calculate the exact price per person. Gregory R. Bennett of the Artemis Project estimates that the full ticket price to the Moon will range between $25,000 and $200,000. His estimate, however, hinges on a number of optimistic premises. For example, that it will be possible to manufacture rocket fuel on the Moon, and that space stations will be orbiting both Earth and the Moon, and that there will be regular flights linking Earth to these stations.

Regular flights from Earth to the space stations will probably be the single most crucial prerequisite for moon tourism, as the laws of physics are not bound to change anytime soon. It takes an enormous amount of energy to escape Earth's field of gravity and to cope with the immense thermal problems of reentry into the atmosphere.

Former NASA employees who have now established their own companies are working on creating single-stage redeployable spacecraft that can be operated the way jet aircraft are, with the aim of keeping liftoff costs below $2 million.

> "If you tell that guy 'C'mon, lets fly to the Moon for a quick cup of coffee,' he'll tell you 'OK, let's go!'"
> *Joseph Beuys about Charles Wilp*

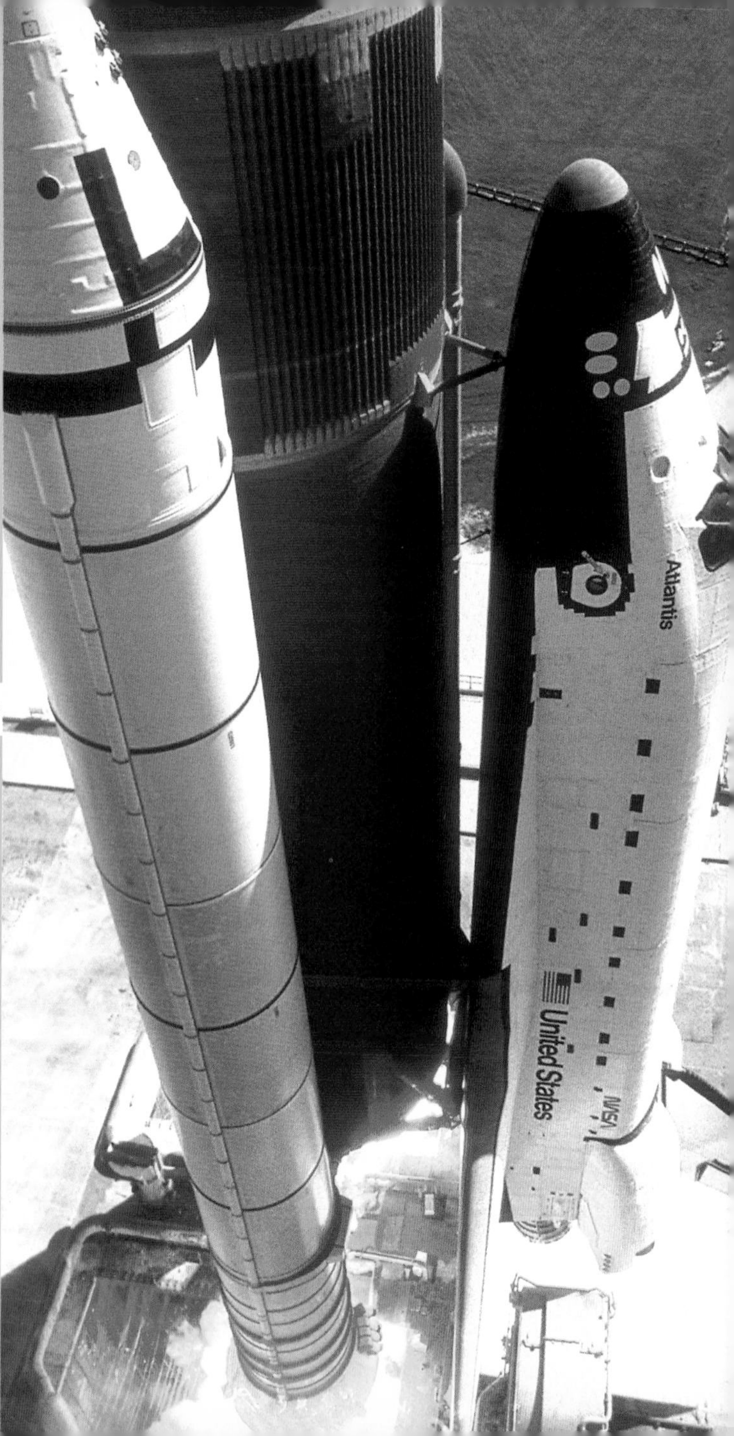
Atlantis
United States
NASA

Preparing for the Trip

Reservations

A trip to the Moon cannot be a spontaneous undertaking. Lunar prebooking has a very long history.

The Three Thousand Volunteers of 1929

On September 30, 1929, Fritz von Opel set off on the first rocket-powered test flight at the old Frankfurt aerodrome. The aircraft was a 300-pound Hatry glider fitted with Sander rockets with an 1,800-pound thrust.

Opel's miracle machine rocketed over the fields of the aerodrome on a shaft of fire until a wind gust smashed it against the ground. Miraculously, the pilot escaped unscathed.

But the dream of rocketing into space was gaining momentum. Mountains of mail flooded into the Opel headquarters: Over three thousand people volunteered to be passengers on the first flight to the Moon.

Five Thousand Adventurers, 1997

The Englishman Thomas Cook invented the package tour in the middle of the nineteenth century — and even back then he already cherished the vision that one day he would be selling tickets to the Moon.

In 1954 his company, Thomas Cook Tours, implemented his idea and set up the first official waiting list for moon flights, the *Moon Register* (not open to North

> "One thing that I remember most vividly was being on the Moon and looking back at the Earth and thinking how far, far away it was. I was impressed by the distance; it seemed very unreal for me to be there. Frequently on the lunar surface I said to myself, 'This is the Moon, that is the Earth. I'm really here. I'm really here.'"
> *Alan Bean* (Apollo 12)

Americans, alas). At the top of the register is Bertrand Cox from Australia, who has passed away, but who took the precaution of insuring that his spot could be passed on to his heirs. Neither Thomas Cook nor the prospective moon tourist is bound by a legal agreement, but the day lunar tours are initiated all the people on the list will be the first in line.

Health

Prerequisites

Average health is all you need for a space flight. To date there is no age limit, but your heart and your blood pressure must be stable. Basic medical reasons for disqualification would be epilepsy, vertigo, obesity, and fear of heights. The most common ailment during weightlessness experienced by even veteran astronauts is a type of nausea similar to seasickness. Your run-of-the-mill antinausea medicine will not be of much use to you.

As with all trips into remote and distant areas, you cannot start preparing yourself early enough.

Test Yourself

A good way of testing your physical and mental capabilities is by trying out parachuting—in the past, an integral part of an astronaut's training. In later stages of space tourism, parachute training will no longer be a prerequisite, but it will still be recommended by specialists.

Deep-sea diving is also a useful form of training. Moving under water is similar to moving in weightlessness, and your body will also accustom itself to pure oxygen, which is what you will be breathing during your moon and space excursions. To date, all astronaut trainees have had to present a professional diver's license before signing up.

Mental Preparation

A strong desire to experience the Moon is almost more important than are physical prerequisites. If you are only tagging along to please a friend or spouse, you would be well advised not to go.

The travails of a trip to the Moon will be more like a daring expedition into uncharted wilds than even the most rough-and-tumble package tour on Earth. Military discipline will be expected of every passenger, and the flight crew's directions will have to be followed completely and unconditionally.

It will be just like being a passenger on a freighter—you are not the main objective of the trip. There will have to be regular flights to the moon base, and if there happens to be space for passengers, then you might be tolerated. But don't expect to be welcomed with open arms: You will be a foreign body in a finely tuned operation, a greenhorn in a professional insider community. Even if you have paid an astronomical sum for your ticket, you cannot count on special treatment. The mental stress of a two-class society rarely will be mentioned but will hover

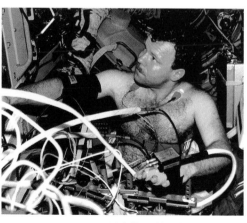

Reinhold Ewald conducting a medical experiment on board the *Mir* space station

"Please don't panic, ladies and gentlemen! It's only Mr. Jackson after his latest operation."

constantly in the background. Long years of military or military-style training will have turned professional astronauts into tough men and women.

Training Camps

Why wait? Excellent facilities to prepare you for space travel already exist. All you need to bring along is regular sportswear (if you will be traveling to the Moon in the future you will need this anyway) and a major credit card. Technical knowledge of space travel is less important. All you need to know about astronaut training you will find in this travel guide.

Space Camp Huntsville

An impressive show is awaiting you in Huntsville, Alabama. The Space and Rocket Center is the biggest space travel museum in the world and houses the official visitor center of the NASA Marshall Space Flight Center.

Here you can see the original rocket in which the first American flew into space, and the mighty *Saturn V*, with which America reached the Moon. In the Space Dome Theater you can watch a mission to Mars in IMAX format.

There is also a flight simulator for the more robust visitor, which will spin you around at 4 g (more than you will experience in a shuttle flight). The new Space Shot simulator will give you a taste of weightlessness.

Space & Rocket Center
One Tranquility Base
Huntsville, AL 35805, USA
Tel: 1-800-63-SPACE
E-mail: resv1@spacecamp.com
Web site:
http://www1.msfc.nasa.gov/

The U.S. Space Academy

For a much more intensive adventure, you can sign up for a three-day space training course at the U.S. Space Academy at Huntsville. A number of trainers prepare groups of participants for a mission, including how to start a space shuttle, how to dock it, how to assemble a satellite frame in space, and, finally, how to land.

All this takes place in various simulators: a shuttle model that simulates the vibrations of liftoff; a Multi-Axis-Trainer in which three axes give you a good rattling while simulating a flat spin; a Five-Degrees-of-Freedom-Chair in which five of the six movement axes of weightlessness are imitated—the sixth, floating freely in a vertical position, is left out.

The Space Academy does not expect trainees to turn into full-fledged astronauts. The whole idea is to have as much fun as possible. Every precaution is taken so that no one is injured, and even out-of-shape and overweight people get their money's worth.

For reservations and information write to or call:

U.S. Space and Rocket Center
Reservations
P.O. Box 070015
Huntsville, AL 35807-7015, USA
Tel: 1-800-533-7281
Fax: 1-256-837-6137
Web site: www.spacecamp.com

Space Camp Titusville

Space Camp Titusville is a theme park in the heart of the NASA Kennedy Space Center in Florida. There is an Astronauts' Hall of Fame, a planetarium, an IMAX theater, and also a spectacular 3D 360-degree Flight Simulator and a special Space-Shuttle Simulator.

A Zero-G-Wall Simulator guarantees that you will experience weightlessness. But for the prime

attraction you have to do some heavy-duty prebooking: In Titusville you can watch, from a polite distance, an actual space shuttle liftoff.

Web site: http://www.spaceport-usa.com

Space Camp Mountain View

The smallest of the three camps belongs to NASA's Ames Research Center in Mountain View, California. The space camp boasts a record: the biggest wind tunnel in the world.

You can stand on a strip of artificial Mars terrain (if you stand in line long enough) and steer a Mars Rover by remote control.

Here, too, there is a Zero-G-Wall Simulator and a Space Station Mobility Trainer, both relatively harmless contraptions in which daring visitors are whirled around a little.

NASA Ames Research Center
Mail Stop 223-3
Moffett Field, CA 9403-1000, USA
Tel: 1-415-604-6497
E-mail:
tourstaff@mail.arc.nasa.gov
Web site:
http://www.arc.nasa.gov/

Star City, Moscow

The Russian cosmonaut space camp is a whole other ball game. It offers more realism and actual classes in theory, and there is less emphasis on fun and games.

The eighteen-day program will take you to the heart of the once top-secret Soviet space program. At the Institute for Medical and Biological Problems for Long Space Flight, your lecturer will be none other than the record-breaking cosmonaut Valery Polyakov, who holds the world record for length of time spent in space. During a trip to St. Petersburg you will visit, among other places, the famous Monino Aeronautics Museum.

The focal point of your stay will be a crash course at the Yuri Gagarin Center, where you will be given an overview of the state-of-the-art program used to train today's cosmonauts. After a brief health check, you will be prepared for life in space with lectures and an array of simulators. In a weightless environment, for instance, the ORLAND space suit will give you some bona fide training in EVA—extravehicular activity.

One of the high points of the program is genuine weightlessness training in a specially equipped Ilyushin IL-76 MDK. At 6,000 meters (19,800 feet) the jet climbs at a 45-degree angle, at which point you are submitted to 2 g of pressure against the floor of the seatless cabin. Then the pilot descends in a 45-degree dive, and during the Ilyushin's subsequent parabolic loop, for twenty-five seconds there is absolute weightlessness in the padded cabin. All the trainees have described this experience as incredible. But after the twenty-five seconds are over, gravity sets in with a bang at 2 g pressure. An instructor sees to it that everyone gets back on the floor of

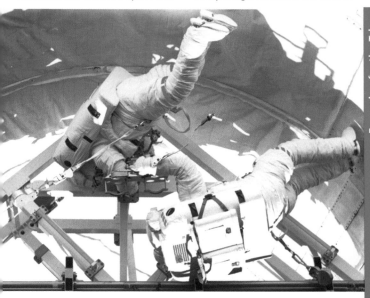

the cabin safely, otherwise serious injuries could occur.

The pilot flies ten parabolic loops in a row, in itself a great endurance test. Quite a few participants make use of the copious supply of paper bags. (In astronaut slang the training jets are known as *barf-bombers*.)

Then there are also the odd nocturnal orientation forays, weather permitting, which typically culminate around a jovial campfire, with soulful Russian songs, and a free-flow of alcohol.

There is a rule at Star City that you can be barred from the program if you overindulge in alcohol. Your hosts, however, will expect you to conform to the local customs and take part in boisterous drinking rounds—otherwise, by Russian standards, you will definitely not qualify as an astronaut.

The crowning event of the program is the awarding of the cosmonaut graduation certificate.

Apollo Aerospace International, Inc.
P.O. Box 11461
Daytona Beach, FL 32120, USA
Tel: 1-904-304-1245
Fax: 1-904-304-3025
E-mail: njsimaos@apollo-
aerospace.com
Web site: www.apollo-
aerospace.com/training_school.html
Price: $7,500

Cité de l'espace, Toulouse

The first European space park was opened on June 28, 1997, in southwest France in Toulouse, the capital of Europe's space-travel industry. Under the sponsorship of the French woman astronaut Claudie André-Deshays, this amusement park offers 140

cultural and educational "interactive elements"—all of them of a scientific nature.

There is a life-size model of the Ariane rocket, a liftoff simulator, a planetarium, 3D movies, a genuine Soyuz capsule, asteroids you can climb about on, and so on.

For European space travel, which could learn a thing or two from NASA's publicity machine, this $20 million theme park is a step in the right direction.

La Cité de l'espace
4 rue Maryse-Hilsz
Toulouse, France
Tel: 011-33-5-62-71-64-80
Web site: www.cite-espace.com

Do-It-Yourself Training

The Oregon Moonbase, near the town of Bend in Oregon, has a

> "They started to put the hatch on. This is the moment when things begin to come home to you. Up to this point people are reaching into the capsule and working all around you and there's no real feeling of being on your own. Suddenly, as people begin to pat you on the shoulder, wink at you, shake your hand and wave good-bye, it changes."
>
> *John Glenn* (Mercury 9)

simple setup to prepare you for the adversities of the lunar landscape. Lava tubes, volcanic dust, and a wide basalt plain offer a striking resemblance to the Moon's terrain. In the past, builders of prototype lunar vehicles used the Oregon Moonbase, sponsored by the Oregon Museum of Science and Industry, as a testing ground.

Other moonlike formations can be found near Mount Saint Helens in Washington state, particularly Ape Cave, and the cave formations of Pinchot National Park in the Nevada desert.

There is also moonlike volcanic terrain in the Canary Islands, in Korea, and in Hawaii on the Big Island, where you can try out your moon suits and other lunar equipment.

For more information, write to:

Oregon L5 Society
P.O. Box 86
Oregon City, OR 97045
USA

Transportation

The method of transportation is pretty much fixed: You will travel in a spacecraft of the:

Space Shuttle Class

Not in one of the three models that have been in service since 1981, but in a quite similar one. However, the enormous amount of time and money needed to develop a new type of craft rules out the possibility that there will be one in the foreseeable future.

In 1972, the United States decided to design a reusable spacecraft to supplant the gigantic single-use rockets of the Apollo program, a decision that held space travel back for at least a decade. All available resources were poured into the single most expensive piece of technology ever to leave the ground. At the peak of activity, in 1977, over fifty thousand people were working on the space shuttle.

Single-Stage Dreams

There have been many plans for other single-stage spacecraft (Single Space To Orbit, SSTO). In California there are quite a few companies with an impressive roster of former NASA engineers toiling away at high-flying constructions, with which they hope to bring down the liftoff costs from today's $60 million to under $2 million.

The shuttles that are in service today can easily cope with the current limited need for manned space research.

But who knows—maybe one day, lunar mining or some other unanticipated enterprise might light a fire under spacecraft development.

The Russian space industry also has its own shuttle, *Buran* (the spitting image of the American prototype), and *Energiya,* the rocket that goes with it. Both are ready and waiting for customers. For the time being, however, the Russian program is on ice due to a chronic lack of funds.

High-Powered Fuel

The shuttle runs on the most effective fuel man has been able to come up with: liquid oxygen and liquid hydrogen. Together they form the highly explosive oxyhydrogen. The oxygen has been chemically treated to stop everything from going up in flames.

And yet there is no substance less practical than hydrogen. For it to liquefy, its temperature has to be brought down to −253°C (−423.4°F). As a result, the tank needs an exorbitantly high-priced insulation system—and the tank needs to be gigantic. Liquid hydrogen is extremely light: 1 liter of liquid hydrogen weighs 66 grams (.23 ounces).

The resulting $15 million monster of a tank is a tower that stands 153.8 feet high and has a diameter of 27.6 feet. The empty two-part tank weighs 32 tons. In its upper tank it can carry 604 tons of liquid oxygen (at a temperature of –183°C [–297.4°F]), and 102 tons of liquid hydrogen in its lower one. The whole tank is much larger than the space shuttle itself and looks like a typical rocket, but it has no engines: The power comes from the shuttle's rocket jets.

After the first ten minutes of flight, the tank has done its job and is jettisoned back to Earth. This expensive piece of high-tech equipment breaks up as it enters Earth's atmosphere and crashes into the sea. It is the final remnant of the former disposable single-use spacecraft.

The Incredible Engine

For a long time it seemed that building the shuttle's rocket engine was technically impossible. The fuel has to be forced into three combustion chambers at an incredible 365 atmospheres (that is, 32 tons on a surface that's the size of a man's palm). The temperature shoots up to 3,500°C (6,332°F). (Steel melts at 1,500°C [2,732°F].)

The miraculous functioning of this system was brought about by means of a clever cooling system. A row of five centrifugal pumps boosts the fuel up to the right pressure. They spin at 37,000 rotations per minute. If a chamber should overheat or a blade break, the whole system would explode.

And yet, this most powerful of all flight engines, with its colossal thrust, is not strong enough to accelerate the immense shuttle quickly enough. Two extra solid-fuel rockets—known as aft solid rocket boosters—are attached to the sides of the tank. They are cheaper than the complicated liquid-fuel propulsion system, but come with a horrifying disadvantage: Once they start burning they cannot be turned off.

Pioneering rocket scientist Wernher von Braun had considered liquid-fuel propulsion systems too dangerous, so they were not used in the Apollo flights. In the *Challenger* tragedy, it was a

In the cockpit of a space shuttle

defective piece of insulation on one of the boosters that led to the explosion of the hydrogen tank.

Flying Cathedrals

The shuttle's two rocket boosters are as tall as a church steeple: 150 feet high and 12 feet in diameter, weighing 586 tons. The propellant is largely aluminum powder, which is distributed so that the rocket's thrust gradually diminishes. If it were to remain constant, the acceleration due to the decrease in weight would be too extreme for the passengers.

The propulsion period of the reusable boosters is about two minutes. Then they are jettisoned into the sea. Even empty, they weigh 80 tons apiece, and their fall has to be buffered by parachutes—the largest in the world.

Before We Fly to the Moon

Before you will have the opportunity to set out for the Moon, there will be a whole slew of other space-travel offers on the market for paying passengers.

The X-Price Foundation was established in memory of Charles Lindbergh, the first man to fly over the Atlantic, in order to give space tourism a powerful boost. X-Price intends to spur private enterprise by establishing a prize for the first company to take private passengers up into space. Peter H. Diamandis, the president of the foundation, aims to open up space travel to everyone.

The current favorite for the X-Price trophy is the Space Cruiser, a craft 18 meters (19.8 yards) long, weighing 12 tons, which can carry two pilots and six passengers into space. The Space Cruiser will be

carried on a transport plane to an altitude of 15 kilometers (9.3 miles) and released. When its rocket engines ignite, the pilot points the craft straight up, and after only two minutes of propulsion it reaches an altitude of 65 kilometers (40.3 miles). The Space Cruiser then flies out into space at three times the speed of sound.

Once the craft has reached space, complete weightlessness sets in, and there is a breathtaking view of Earth. You will be grabbed by what is known in astronaut circles as the "overview effect"—the indescribable euphoria one experiences when one sees Earth's globe far below and feels completely removed from earthly worries.

But the fun is short-lived. After only two and a half minutes, the pilot fires the brake ignition, the Space Cruiser reenters Earth's atmosphere with a jolt, and then lands like a regular jet after having been airborne for only two and one half hours. During the rocket thrust and the braking phase, passengers are subjected to a moderate 2 g of pressure.

The trip will cost you $98,000, which includes a one-week stay at a training camp, where you will have to undergo extensive theoretical and practical astronaut training. As a bonus, you get to keep your space suit and are given the video of the flight recorded by the minicamcorder built into your helmet.

The tour has been set up by Zegrahm, which specializes in "extreme" vacations, ranging from Mount Everest to Antarctica. Thirty passengers have already signed up, and the first flight is scheduled for December 1, 2001.

Zegrahm Space Voyages
1414 Dexter Avenue N. #2001
Seattle, WA 98109, USA
Fax: 1-206-285-7390
Web site:
www.SpaceVoyages.com

There is another similar project in the works in which NASA has joined forces with Lockheed Martin. The X-34 craft will take off strapped to the back of a jumbo jet, and test flights have already been scheduled for 1999. Its successor, the X-33, will be able to lift off vertically like a space shuttle.

Both these craft have been designed with the idea of taking satellites into orbit, but they can

David Scott and *Apollo 15*'s lunar rover

be fitted easily enough with passenger cabins. The current cargo price of approximately $17,000 per kilogram is projected to drop to a mere $1,500.

Colorado's Pioneer Rocketplane Company and the U.S. Air Force have joined forces to build *Pathfinder*, a rocket plane similar to the shuttle.

Pathfinder will take off like a regular jet and then rendezvous with a tanker aircraft at an altitude of 20,000 feet, which will transfer to it approximately 130,000 pounds of liquid oxygen. Then the *Pathfinder*'s RD-120 rocket engines will take it to an altitude of 70 miles above Earth at 21,500 kilometers per hour (13,330 miles per hour), eighteen times the speed of sound.

Pathfinder's main task will be to take satellites into orbit. But the project of transporting up to forty passengers to various terrestrial destinations with great speed is also on the agenda. A trip from New York to London would take just under half an hour, and as a bonus one would get a breathtaking vista of Earth—and even five minutes of weightlessness.

Vacation in Space

Tourism plays an important part in most financial projections for future space travel. Once the International Space Station is up and running, paying customers will be able to visit for short periods. Marketing strategists predict that initially large companies will sponsor lotteries for trips to the space station, and later to the Moon.

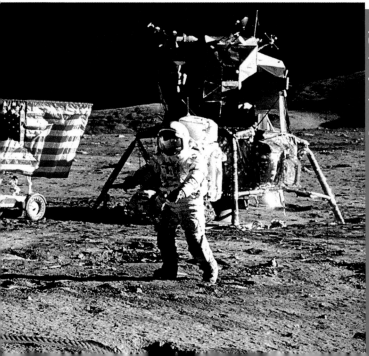

Tips from A to Z

Alcohol

Wine, beer, and alcohol in general are taboo in space. Unlike the astronauts on previous missions, you will not be personally responsible for the success of the trip—but you will be expected to sign a legal document agreeing to adhere to all the rules during the flight.

Should there ever be cause for celebration in space, glasses of mineral water and jugs of alcohol-free beer will be raised. There have been rumors that cosmonauts did manage to smuggle the odd vodka bottle onto the space station—but this has never been officially confirmed.

Diplomatic Representation

In 1980, Dennis Hope handed in a claim at the San Francisco Land Registry Office for ownership of the Moon. After some back and forth, the director of the office accepted Hope's petition but specified a lengthy period in which the state could file an objection to the petition.

Shortly thereafter, Hope founded the diplomatic mission to the Moon and informed the United Nations, as well as the Russian government, that he was intending to sell plots of land on the Moon. No country contested Hope's claim within the specified period.

Hope has proclaimed himself the greatest landowner of the solar system.

The Lunar Embassy
6000 Airport Road
Rio Vista, CA 94571, USA
Web site: www.moonshop.com

Electricity

For safety reasons, only low-voltage electricity is available on spaceships, space stations, and space shuttles. Astronauts recommend using a charger for electric appliances. There can, however, be problems with chargers for camcorders, which would need a special adapter.

The Founding of Nations

In the wake of people who have bought property on the Moon from Dennis Hope, it was only to be expected that the owners would attempt to establish nations on the Moon.

The first, according to current information, would be the *Owli Cave Lunar Republic,* founded by Lit Caveman, who unfortunately does not reveal his earthly name. He owns a parcel near the Crater Tycho and is certain that his property contains at least one cave.

The Crest of the Owli Cave Lunar Moon Republic

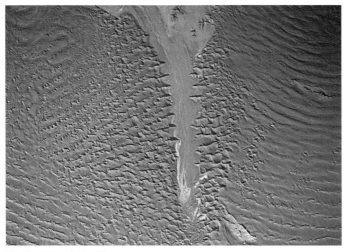
The Namib Desert, Namibia

That's why he named his land Owli Cave. Caveman welcomes every intelligent form of life (whether human or not) as inhabitants.

On November 4, 1997, Lit Caveman and the Japanese owner of moon property Ylum proclaimed the Alliance of United Moon Republics. The Japanese owner is speculating on someday selling the surface mining rights on his property to the Japanese mining concern Mintaka, which has already expressed interest in the mineral treasures of the Moon.

In February 1998, the Polish newspaper *Gazeta Wyborcza* raffled off fifty moon lots, all in the Crater Tycho, which means that there will be a Polish quarter on the Moon. That added fifty potential settlers to Owli Cave's alliance, who, at the request of the newspaper, are already developing various proposals for constitutions for their own republics.

In the summer of 1998 the Japanese pop singer Kyoko Date was made an honorary citizen of Owli Cave. The trip to the Moon will not present any problems for her, since Kyoko (just like the adventuress Lara Croft) is a "virtual figure," completely created by computer.

Meanwhile, Caveman's call has called forth a powerful response. According to his report, over four thousand lunar lot proprietors have joined the Owli Cave Lunar Republic. On August 2, 2002, the constitutional congress will convene. Dennis Hope, as acknowledged owner of the Moon, has been invited to give the principal address, although there is a lot of irritation among the citizens about his dictatorial Bill of Rights. The future political development of the Moon will be interesting—luckily we won't have to take it too seriously for now (www.polbox.com/o/owlicave).

Fun and games

A timid attempt to found another United Lunar Republic was made on December 1, 1998, by a certain President Tokie (http://members. xoom.com/ulr).

We can count on further attempts and interesting negotiations.

Fun and Games

A small warning about gambling on the Moon. Due to the Moon's low gravity, objects fall more slowly, and certain movements come across in slow motion. Throw a coin on the Moon, and you can see which way it is going to fall. Hoodwinking an opponent as the dice roll is a snap.

Hotels

Be prepared at the beginning for Spartan quarters. Only after the pioneering phase will improvement be in sight: The Hilton Hotels group already has plans for a Lunar Hilton in the drawer.

In 1998, for $300,000 the hotel chain commissioned the British architect Peter Inston to prepare a study, and he outdid himself: five thousand beds, and at a height of 325 meters (1,066 feet), the building will be a few meters taller than the Eiffel Tower. Inston's plan includes restaurants, an enormous infirmary, landing pads for

Mars

Venus

Saturn

space shuttles, an ecumenical church, a school, countless high-speed elevators, and a swimming pool in the front of a lake with shore plantings, fed by the Moon's plentiful supply of water.

The whole building is a gigantic pressurized cabin, and the architect has even thought of extra-heavy shoes for the guests, so that they "will be better able to cope with the weaker gravity."

The Lunar Hilton will doubtless have to be counted among the large group of "publicity stunts," a technique that is especially popular with Japanese construction firms. The Shimizu concern has published plans for inflatable moon buildings with their own tennis courts and golf courses. The construction giant Nishimatu entered the field with a resort community consisting of three ten-story buildings in the form of snail shells—all of which are lacking even the minimal protection against radiation.

Insurance
Life
You definitely need to plan ahead. A preliminary survey of various insurance companies indicates that space travel (even if it is taken up by the tourist industry) will be classified as a high-risk sport.

In other words, should you take out a policy before you set off for the Moon, it would be termed invalid in case of an accident. Preexisting life insurance policies, on the other hand (policies that have been taken out a minimum of two years prior to travel), are legally binding. If worst comes to the worst, the money will be paid to your heirs.

Medical
Your regular health insurance will not cover space travel. Therefore, all medical coverage during your flight to the Moon and your stay there will be included in the fare.

Cancellation
In view of the high costs, the limited number of passengers, and the high risk factor in space travel, no insurance company will be prepared to foot the bill for a passenger wishing to cancel at short notice.

A suggestion that came up at the Congress of Space Travel was that a NASA practice could be implemented: With every group there could be a number of stand-by passengers ready to step in in case of cancellations. These passengers could then travel at a slight discount.

Jupiter

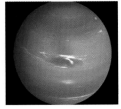
Neptune

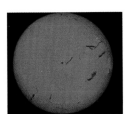
Sun

Language

The official languages in space are English and Russian. In the event that the Russian space program will also offer tourist trips, English will be employed as a second language. Prepare yourself for the Russians' creative approach to English.

Money

In space you won't have much use for cash. Take your credit cards. Once hotel-like moon bases are up and running, you can shop till you drop with credit cards. In the early stages of space tourism, the organizers might well require a deposit for optional outings, drinks, etc.

Moon money® has been available in the United States since the middle of 1998. Please be aware that it is not the official currency for the Moon, but is, according to Cynthia Peden at http://www.moonmoney.com, a low-cost investment that an average individual can afford.

According to Peden, placing silver coins on the windowsill is a "very ancient prosperity folk tradition. Some say it's Polish, others say it's Hungarian, Chinese or Celtic."

On this Web site you can purchase a "vintage silver coin, 1964 or earlier," for ten dollars.

http://www.moonmoney.com

Real Estate

You can purchase plots of land at the Lunar Embassy (see "Diplomatic Representation," above). For $15.99, plus $11.16 moon tax and

Tiki's lunar plot

handling, you will be mailed a lunar deed naming you owner of 1,777.58 acres of moon territory. The head of the Lunar Embassy, Dennis Hope, guarantees that all plots are on the near side of the Moon with a prime view of Earth.

Needless to say, the author owns a lunar plot, and when the time comes he will throw a big party there for our readers.

Buyers wishing to set their sights higher can purchase terrain for a whole lunar city. Nineteen such zones are available at $4,500 each, made up of two hundred adjacent plots of land.

All lunar-city zones lie within easy reach of American and Russian landing sites. You can give your lunar city the name of your choice. There are already zones reserved for Lunafornia, Tycho City, and New Berlin.

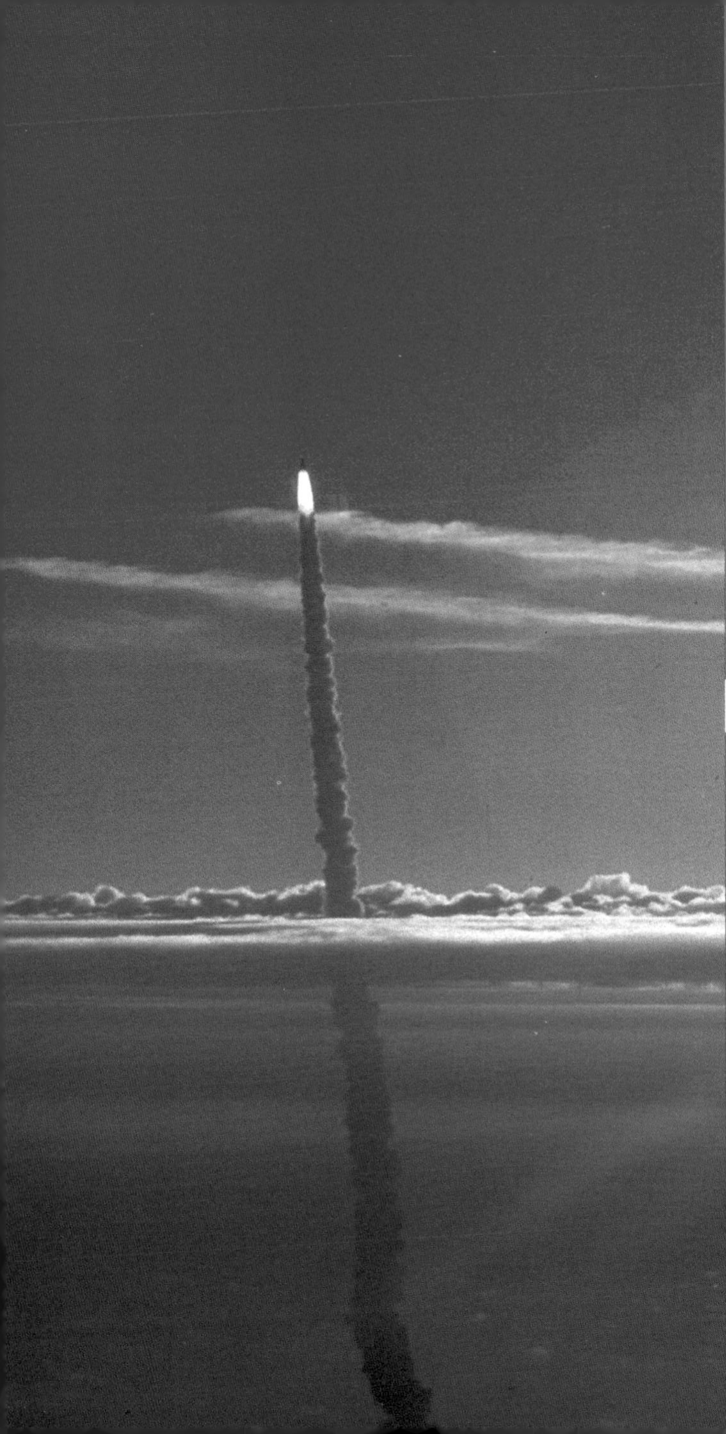

Smoking

You will be allowed to smoke only before liftoff and after you return to Earth. During the flight and your stay on the Moon you will have to find other ways of dealing with your nerves. The smoke of cigarettes, cigars, and pipes would immediately disable the air regenerators.

Russian cosmonauts are said to have turned at times to tobacco-chewing on the space station. But before you could begin chewing, you first would have to get the consent of your fellow passengers—and in a larger tour group you will have your work cut out for you.

Special Events

On Earth there is a partial solar eclipse from two to five times a year: The Moon moves between the Sun and Earth and casts a shadow on the Earth's surface.

A total solar eclipse happens very seldom; when it does, the Moon hides the solar disc completely, and in a certain area on Earth darkness falls in the middle of the day. The last such eclipse took place in 1842, and in 1999 we will have another one: On August 11, this spectacular event can be seen from within an 80-kilometer-wide (50 miles)

strip, stretching from Germany to the Black Sea. At about 12:40 P.M., darkness will fall on Munich, where the Olympia Tower viewers can watch the eclipse approaching from far away. The eclipse itself will last two minutes and twenty seconds, until the full moon shadow has passed over the viewers.

This spectacle will be a good reason to fly to Europe in the summer of 1999. And your next chance won't come until October 7, 2135.

From the Moon you can experience these solar eclipses as terrestrial eclipses: You will see a dark spot on Earth moving slowly from west to east.

Even more spectacular are the lunar eclipses (which from the Moon can be viewed as solar eclipses), when the Earth fully covers the Moon. Depending on which part of the Moon you will be watching the eclipse from, you can view a partial or a complete eclipse of the Sun.

During a total eclipse, Earth's atmosphere creates a spectacular orange-red haze around the dark side of Earth. This spectacle lasts up to three and a half hours, and throughout it the ring of fire grows until it completely surrounds

Solar Eclipses on the Moon
(Seen from Earth as lunar eclipses)

January 21, 2000	total eclipse
January 9, 2001	total
May 16, 2003	total
November 9, 2003	total
May 4, 2004	total
October 28, 2004	total
September 7, 2006	partial eclipse
March 3, 2007	total
February 21, 2008	total
August 16, 2008	partial
December 31, 2009	partial
December 21, 2010	total
June 15, 2011	total
December 10, 2011	total
May 26, 2021	total
November 19, 2021	partial
May 16, 2022	total
September 8, 2022	total
October 28, 2023	partial
November 18, 2024	partial
March 14, 2025	total
September 7, 2025	total
March 3, 2026	total
August 28, 2026	partial
January 12, 2028	partial
July 6, 2028	partial
December 31, 2028	total
June 26, 2029	total
December 20, 2029	total
June 15, 2030	partial

Earth. Then the Moon, too, is almost completely steeped in darkness, except for a glowing reddish haze that covers the lunar landscape.

The lunar eclipse can also be seen from Earth's dark side, and with a good telescope you can observe the weak reddish glow Earth casts onto the lunar surface.

So that you do not miss this sensational spectacle, check the following list of eclipses.

Taxes

All prices will include taxes applicable in the tour's country of origin.

An interesting question will be whether trips into space will qualify as tax deductions. No doubt the IRS will consider any such deductions on a case-by-case basis. If you can prove that the main objective of your trip is to conduct business, there should be no problem. But be sure to check with your tax consultant before liftoff.

Time Zones

In space, the Universal Time Code (UTC) is in effect — previously known as GMT, Greenwich Mean Time, the Zero Time Zone in which London lies. During the journey,

you will be set on an artificial sleeping and waking cycle, which will be specifically calculated for each trip so passengers feel fresh and alert upon arrival on the Moon.

Tipping

For space travel we suggest the time-honored cruise-ship practice: Before liftoff the flight crew should be given a set tip (unofficially). The crew of the space station and the moon base should also be taken care of on arrival. This will free you from having to worry about such minor details during your stay.

Vertigo

When on the Moon, you don't have to balk at steep rocks and ravines. On Earth, when an object falls from a height of 2 meters (6.6 feet), it takes 0.6 seconds and impacts at around 22 kilometers per hour (13.6 miles per hour). On the Moon the same object takes 1.6 seconds to fall and lands at a comfortable 9 kilometers per hour (5.6 miles per hour).

This radical difference becomes clearer when you think of it this way: On Earth you can jump off a 2-meter (6.6-feet) wall easily enough with a bit of practice. The average person's legs can cushion a fall at 22 kilometers per hour (13.6 miles per hour). On the Moon you could jump off a 12-meter (39.6 feet) cliff and land with the same impact— that's like jumping from a five-story building!

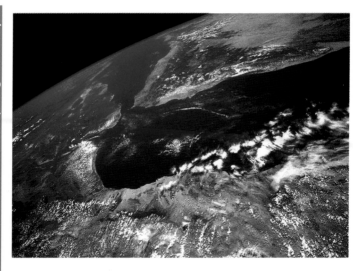

The Voyage

To the Starting Line

Spaceports invariably lie near the equator so that the shuttles can use the power of the Earth's rotation for additional momentum at liftoff. The Artemis Project of the industrious Lunar Resources Group recommends the north Australian island Groote Eylandt for liftoff because of the increasing opposition of nature conservationists at the customary launch pads in Florida and California.

The Russian space industry, too, is planning to negotiate a long-term lease for a launch pad in Australia. In a nutshell, before traveling into space you might well have to undertake a lengthy terrestrial journey.

Needless to say, family and friends wishing to experience the spectacular liftoff and, if necessary, to hold your hand during the pretrip preparation time, will be welcome to join you for the first leg of the trip.

Ground Training

At the liftoff area you will be initiated into the particularities of space travel. You should count on at least a week's preparation. There will be a string of medical examinations, and you will be forced to live practically under military conditions. Your sleeping and waking hours, for instance, will be set to match the artificial day and night cycles on the spacecraft, and your nutrition will be set so that your body can adjust itself to the unusual astronaut diet.

This is particularly important for liftoff, where clean bowels are recommended—as a precaution, you will have to wear a form of adult diaper to face the extreme acceleration pressure of liftoff.

Travel Wear

Cloth fibers and dirt floating around in the atmosphere on board can damage sensitive instruments. As a result, you will be supplied with outfits made of fiberless and non-flammable elastic material in a special decontaminated chamber before boarding. These outfits will have many pockets, as it would be dangerous for objects to be floating around in the cabin during periods of weightlessness. You will have to wear a special pressure suit over this outfit, at least during the early phases of space tourism. During liftoff you will have to wear a sealed helmet with a separate oxygen supply. This has become an international prerequisite since the 1986 *Challenger* disaster—should there be a fire on board, you would still have a chance to survive.

Liftoff

The passage from the terminal to the rocket will remain etched forever in your memory. Even if you don't have to march past the gigantic carrier-rocket's hissing jets, as the pioneers of space travel had to, it is unlikely you will ever forget this walk through the security tunnel into the spacecraft.

Your pulse will rise to two and a half times normal. Be prepared for psychological stress. Every astronaut is plagued by destructive thoughts during this walk: "What am I getting myself into?" — "I can still turn back!" — "I must have been crazy to let them talk me into this!" This is a normal crisis in the everyday life of an astronaut.

Boarding

On shuttle flights, boarding takes place relatively close to liftoff, as the gigantic tank is filled with liquid oxygen and hydrogen at the very last moment in order to keep down the loss of fuel through evaporation.

Notwithstanding extensive insulation, large amounts of fuel keep vaporizing and must be continually replenished during the liftoff phase. Hydrogen boils at −245°C (−409°F) and the resulting fumes give the area around the gigantic spaceport an unforgettable aura.

You will be led to a contour seat specially adapted to fit your body, where you will be literally fettered

into place with numerous seat belts. Then the cabin door will be locked and bolted.

Don't be surprised if the craft sways a little. Once the support frame has been removed from the gigantic carrier rocket, a passenger's abrupt movement is enough to make the whole shuttle sway.

Diabolical Din

You will be given large ear protectors through which you will be able to listen to the countdown. At zero, you will feel a powerful jolt coming from the solid fuel rockets, and, immediately afterwards, the jets beneath the shuttle will ignite. Multistage pumps will force a mixture of liquid oxygen and hydrogen at immense pressure into the three combustion chambers.

Despite the sound-insulation systems and the ear protectors, you will hear a tremendous rattling and howling.

The sound level outside is 160 decibels, the maximum noise a man-made machine has ever managed to make. Your hearing will be put under immense strain — a side effect of rocket science that will doubtlessly be glossed over in the tour brochures.

Next the whole craft starts shaking so violently that you might well think the worst is about to happen. For at least five seconds after ignition the craft is held down by gigantic clamps. Only when the full thrust of 2,800 tons has been reached does the hold-down system release the

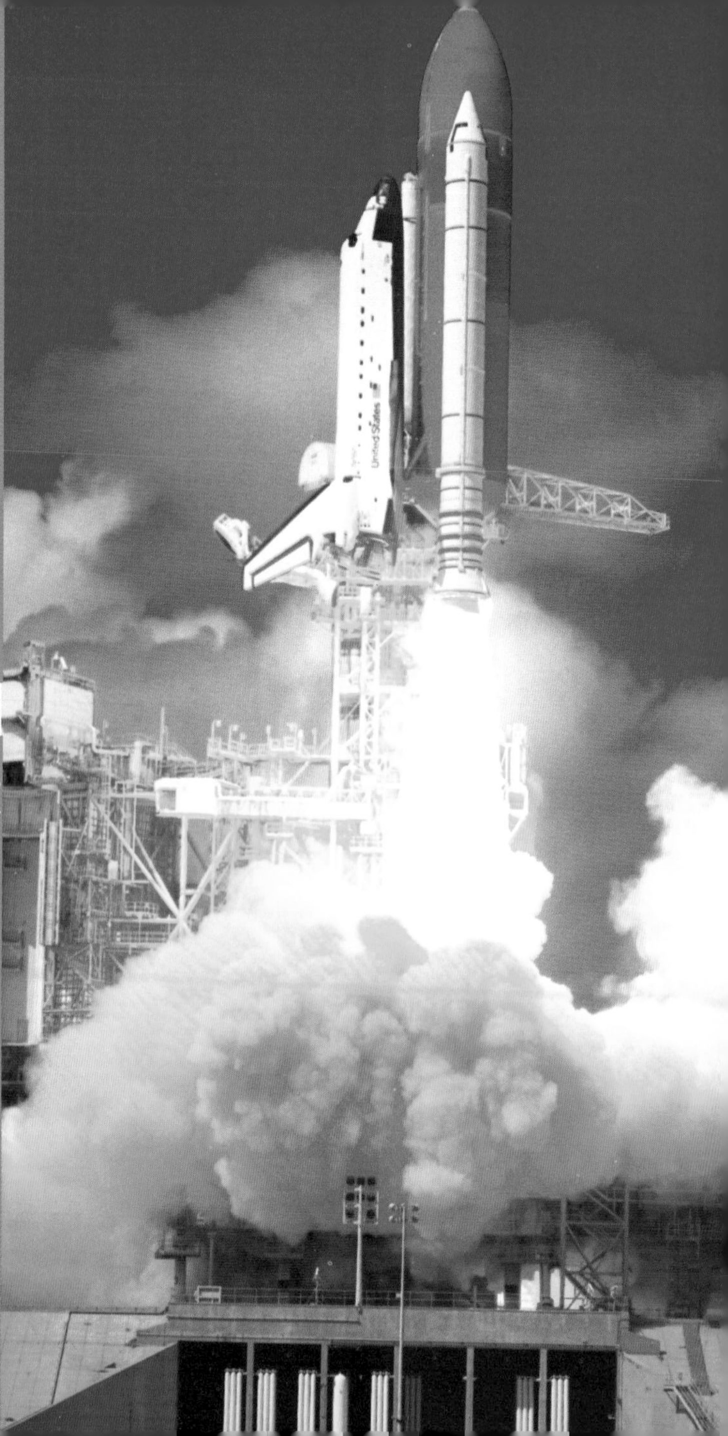
United States

craft, which then begins rising like an elevator.

Breaking the Sound Barrier

Initially the liftoff seems easy enough, slow and majestic. But the acceleration keeps mounting, and you will be pressed harder and harder into your seat. In less than sixty seconds, the shuttle breaks the sound barrier. The strong shaking begins again as the shuttle is exposed to maximum dynamic pressure. Air friction heats the shuttle's nose to 1,500°C (2,732°F).

Once the sound barrier has been broken, the air resistance begins to slacken and the unbearable noise begins to subside a little. The shuttle also becomes lighter—it burns 9 tons of fuel per second.

The thrust of the carrier rockets diminishes, but the craft continues to accelerate. After two minutes, you will be pressed into your seat at three times the Earth's gravity (3 g), the maximum an average person can endure. If you are grappling for a comforting thought at this point, how about this: In early space flights, astronauts had to endure an anguishing 6 g at liftoff and were trained to survive it in gigantic centrifuges. Many otherwise superb trainees were disqualified at this stage.

The first American astronaut in space, Alan Shepard (he later also flew to the Moon in *Apollo 14*), had to endure an inhuman 11 g at touchdown. Back then it was taken for granted that astronauts became unconscious during reentry into the atmosphere.

In Space

In the meantime you will have reached an altitude of 30 miles, and suddenly the pressure subsides. The two aft solid rocket boosters will be jettisoned with a loud bang, and the shuttle will fly on with its external tank and rocket jets.

Slowly the pressure will start to rise again, and after about five minutes of constant acceleration the strain will become hard to bear for even the toughest among you.

It is not clear if a shuttle's passenger cabin will be able to have windows that won't have to be sealed from outside during the intense pressures of liftoff. If, however, you were able to look out, you would now see the endless darkness of the universe.

Only after nine minutes, which without a doubt will seem much longer to you, is the external tank also jettisoned, and then, in a flash, weightlessness sets in.

"Coming across the Pacific we were given a 'go' for translunar insertion. We fired the engine and it was just like we were in a gigantic elevator that was lifted straight up. I looked out my window and there, framed beautifully right in the center, were the Hawaiian Islands. All the while we were being lifted up majestically, accelerating to 25,000 miles an hour."
James Irwin (Apollo 15)

In Orbit

After nine minutes and twenty seconds you are in space. You are now hurtling around Earth at 27,000 kilometers per hour (16,740 miles per hour), at an altitude of 240 kilometers (149 miles). The spacecraft is in a free-falling mode, but because it is traveling at such a high altitude and speed, it stays in a perfect orbit rather than plunging back to Earth.

Weightless!

As weightlessness sets in, your arms begin floating upward as if of their own volition. Your whole body shifts into a different mode. Your face becomes fuller, and wrinkles disappear because your blood is no longer being pulled downward by gravity. Your feet also become smaller and you will have to tighten your shoelaces. Your waist becomes slimmer, and you will ultimately gain up to three centimeters in height because your spinal cord is no longer compressed. This is the reason you had to put on elastic clothing.

Now you can help each other wriggle out of the amorphous pressure suits and enjoy the incredible view of Earth.

If you happen to be looking down onto the dark side of Earth, you will be surprised to see that even the brightest city lights are no longer visible from this height.

> "It really hit us when we turned around and looked at the Earth. From the time that it took us for the burn until we got around to see Earth again it had started to shrink. We were on our way to the Moon."
> *James Lovell Jr.* (Apollo 8, 13)

Once your eyes have accustomed themselves to the darkness, you will notice that there are always electric storms raging somewhere on our planet: This is an incredible spectacle that has awed every astronaut.

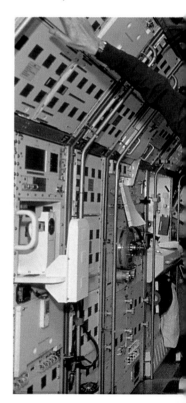

Ulrich Walter in the Spacelab

Space Station Earth

It is very unlikely that you will fly nonstop to the Moon like the daredevil Apollo pioneers did. There will almost certainly be a stopover at a space station.

The primary reasons for this are economic. Boosting the heavy space shuttle with the amount of acceleration it would need to reach the Moon would take too much fuel to be practical. So after a short stopover at the space station, you will board an outlandish-looking moon shuttle. As there is no need for aerodynamics in space, all the blueprints for these models have a predominant Star Trek appearance.

Attractions at 240 Kilometers (149 Miles) Up

An orbiting space station offers the comfort level of a house trailer, as the compact interior is designed for maximum practicality with everything in its designated place. You will have to follow strict rules, and it is quite likely that your quarters will be separate from those of the scientists and astronauts working on board.

But the American tour organizers will undoubtedly come up with

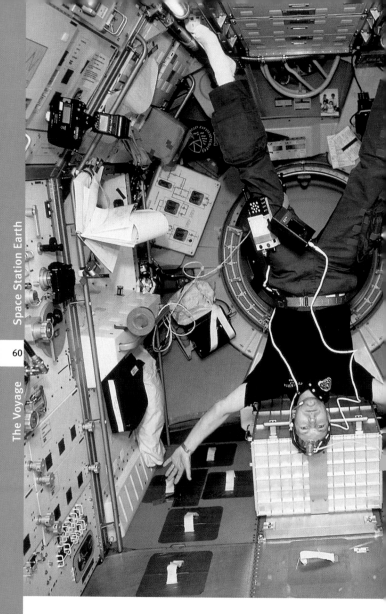

an idea or two to turn your stay into an adventure.

Good music through your earphones will double the effect of the extraordinary view of Earth revolving beneath you. Groups visiting space museums can ask you questions via satellite, and you will have a last opportunity to place a couple of relatively

The Journey to the Moon

Now it is time to board the lunar transfer vehicle (LTV). It pulls away from the space station with extreme caution so as not to shift it out of balance. Watching the gigantic station float weightless in space, slowly turning into a minute dot against the backdrop of the pitch-black universe, is overwhelming.

Good-Bye Earth

The LTV's jets ignite at a safe distance from the space station so as not to disturb the experiments being conducted there. The relatively mild acceleration boost lasts a few minutes and propels the LTV out of Earth's orbit, setting it on its course for the Moon. In the airlessness of space there are neither aerodynamic nor thermal problems.

Now you are gliding practically soundlessly and without thrust through space.

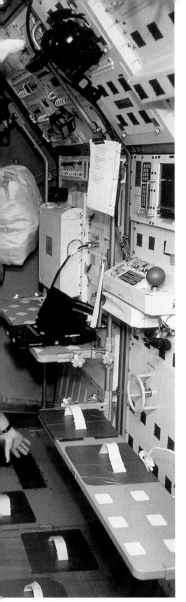

Hans Schlegel in the Spacelab, with an ultrasound measuring instrument strapped to his forehead

low-cost calls to your friends back on Earth.

"It was a totally different Moon than I had ever seen before. The Moon that I knew from old was a yellow flat disk, and this was a huge three-dimensional sphere, almost a ghostly blue-tinged sort of pale white. It didn't seem like a very friendly or welcoming place. It made one wonder whether we should be invading its domain or not."
Michael Collins (Apollo 11)

"You jumped too hard! Now Ethel's in orbit!"

Most of the plans for the lunar transfer vehicle promise you a good view of Earth as it grows smaller in the distance—a powerful and frightening view that no space traveler is ever likely to forget. Through the windows on the other side, you can watch the approaching Moon.

The trip takes two and a half days and is still the longest journey man has ever made into space. You can now relax on board and count your lucky stars if boredom sets in and there are not any sudden technical emergencies.

Space Walks

You might well have the opportunity (for an additional charge) to don a pressure suit, slip through an airlock out into space, and float for a few minutes next to the craft.

This is always an especially dangerous venture because of meteorites, but it is also an extremely powerful experience—and for everyone, even the passengers inside, the ultimate photo-op.

The craft will be flying at a speed of almost 40,000 kilometers per hour (24,800 miles per hour), slowing down only slightly as it comes within the range of the Moon's gravity.

There is a zone between Earth and the Moon in which the gravitational fields of both celestial bodies are equalized. By the late eighteenth century, the French mathematician Joseph Louis

"What amazed me most was silence. Inconceivable silence that could never be heard on Earth. Silence so deep and complete that you begin to hear your own body: Your heart fighting and the veins pulsing, you even hear your muscles rustle when you move them. And in the sky there were more stars than I ever could have imagined."
Soviet Cosmonaut Alexei Leonov, the first human to hover free in space

LaGrange had already determined five points in which the gravitational pull of the Sun is also neutralized. It would be possible to place an immovable satellite or space station at one of these LaGrange points.

The Approaching Moon

At a distance of 10,000 kilometers (6,200 miles), you can still see the entire Moon. But now it is quite clearly a globe, not the flat disk we see from Earth.

Because of the lack of atmosphere, the Moon stands out sharply against the pitch-black universe.

At 1,000 kilometers (620 miles), even if you press your nose hard against the window, only three-quarters of the Moon is visible, and at 200 kilometers (124 miles), as the brake ignition fires, barely a quarter can be seen. The curve of the Moon is much more conspicuous than the curve of Earth from the same distance.

There are various descriptions of the Moon's color. Most visitors have characterized it as a dark metallic gray that takes on first a brownish and then a yellowish brown tint as the sunlight increases, turning almost white when the Sun shines directly onto it.

It is not surprising that accounts differ so much, as one never gets to see the Moon through clear glass. Filters on all the windows of the space station and the spacecraft, as well as helmet visors, protect one's eyes from the intense ultraviolet rays and other dangerous elements.

Moon rock looks very dark in terrestrial light. The Moon's albedo (reflectivity) is an average of 0.07 — in other words, 7 percent of the impacting sunlight is reflected. The dark lunar oceans have an albedo of only 0.03, whereas snow has an albedo of 0.70 and the light granite of the Alps, 0.35. The Moon owes its shine to the completely unfiltered rays of the Sun.

Extreme Desert

If you have ever been in a terrestrial desert, then you will be less amazed at the diversity and color of the monotonous and dead lunar landscape. And yet you will see

"The Earth reminded us of a Christmas tree ornament hanging in the blackness of space. As we got further and further away it diminished in size. Finally it shrank to the size of a marble, the most beautiful marble you can imagine. That beautiful, warm, living object looked so fragile, so delicate, that if you touched it with a finger it would crumble and fall apart. Seeing this has to change a man, has to make a man appreciate the creation of God and the love of God."

James Irwin (Apollo 15)

why all the astronauts fell silent in amazement at the sight of this otherworldly realm.

According to David Scott, commander of *Apollo 15,* the countless meteorite impacts of every size have given the Moon a violent aspect—a chessboard with the marks of a war lasting billions of years. And yet, according to others, the velvety blanket of dust makes the Moon seem gentle and serene.

Trapped by the Moon

As it descends to the Moon, the lunar transfer vehicle turns around and is slowed down to 5,600 kilometers per hour (3,472 miles per hour) by its brake ignition. That is still five times the speed of sound and, from this height, you will have a dynamic view of the craters, oceans, and lunar mountains.

The view is so stunning that your craft will undoubtedly orbit

the Moon once or twice more than is necessary. A complete orbit takes about two hours.

Particularly spectacular is the crossing of the Terminator, the harsh lunar border between light and darkness. On the side facing Earth, the dark portion of the Moon is dipped in the pallid light Earth reflects. On the far side, the Moon is completely black, blacker than the universe in which the unreachable stars shine intensely.

Life in Space

Eating and Drinking

Life in total weightlessness takes some getting used to. A careless move and you can go flying through the cabin, banging your head on a wall or ceiling. You must move very carefully at first, maneuvering yourself from one of the many handgrips to the next.

Dangerous Crumbs

Food is particularly tricky. Luckily, the human swallowing mechanism can work perfectly well without gravity, but liquids cannot be poured and will not stay put in a cup. Cutlery simply floats away.

There must be no crumbs or droplets when you eat—they, too, would go floating through the cabin, doing all kinds of damage. So all liquid nutrition is kept in sealed plastic pouches and squirted into the mouth through a valved tube.

Dining—Light and Lively

Luckily for you, much has changed since the early days of space travel, when the astronauts' food was outrageously inedible. Researchers have discovered in the meantime that heavy sauces tend not to float through the cabin but stick to the food. As a result, certain courses can even be eaten with a knife and fork.

But all nutrition has to be desiccated for preservation and storage. To rehydrate the food, hot water is squirted into the food pouches with a high-tech water pistol. This sounds much less

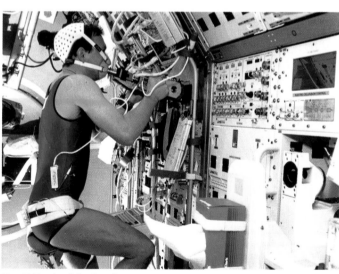

Hans Schlegel pedaling for science

appetizing than it actually is. The meals in the little see-through pouches look quite charming and have been given good ratings by the astronauts. There are hamburgers, sandwiches, desserts— everything with a thin coating of gelatin to keep the crumbs from floating away.

As you eat, you have to take careful bites and chew scrupulously with your mouth shut, so that bits of food do not escape.

Good-Bye to Health Food

There are many reasons why "normal" food is out of the question in space. In a weightless environment the human body has a hard time retaining minerals, and these have to be artificially supplemented in the food. In other words, you will

have to eat up all your veggies, otherwise malnutrition will set in with dire consequences.

During the return journey of the failed *Apollo 13* mission, the astronauts had to make do with a diminished supply of nutrition and fluids. One of them began exhibiting symptoms of severe potassium deficiency even before touchdown, with fever, shivering, and extreme fatigue.

"I was looking down at dark ground, and there was Earthshine. It was like looking at a snow-covered Earth scene under a full Moon."
Ken Mattingly (Apollo 16, Columbia 4, Discovery 3)

Intimate Details

Using a rest room in a weightless environment can present problems of a delicate nature. There are strict procedures, which NASA has classified under "Personal Hygiene," and a legion of crafty contraptions have been developed, which can be viewed at the Air and Space Museum in Washington, D.C.

Vacuum Toilets

The space shuttle's toilet has thigh clamps and handgrips to help you keep yourself firmly positioned on the toilet seat. A powerful ventilator sucks all the waste into a holding tank, where it is disinfected and dried.

To urinate, passengers have to slip on a vacuum-cleaner-like hose that protrudes from the bottom front of the toilet. Here, too, a ventilator vacuums everything away.

A rumor has spread that the shuttle's toilet waste is recycled into the water supply system. Not true! The fuel cells that produce the electricity on board create more than enough water as a by-product.

Sponge Baths

One thing that has remained impracticable has been showering

Maintenance work on the air-conditioning system

in a weightless environment. Time and again shower units have leaked, and large amounts of water floating through the air can be a great hazard for the shuttle's electrical system. It will be far more practical for you to wash with a nondegradable sponge.

A suction pump at the bottom of the funnel-shaped washbasin vacuums the water down into a tank, which is periodically emptied out into space.

Hopefully your nose is not oversensitive. The stench in the close quarters of a spacecraft has not been widely advertised, but former astronauts, now no longer on the space program's payroll, are quite vocal about the many odors that the filtering systems on board seem incapable of eradicating. And it is not just run-of-the-mill human odors, but also the powerful odors of the artificial atmosphere in the space stations and shuttles.

This atmosphere, by the way, which resembles Earth's atmosphere in its makeup, is a great improvement over the pure but highly explosive air that the Apollo astronauts had to breathe.

Sex in Space?

The German astronaut and physicist Ulrich Walter reported that in space one experiences a marked slump in one's libido. The body's hormonal balance has first of all to adapt to the new extreme environment: "During our ten-day shuttle flight we thought of everything, except that one thing." American astronauts have preferred to duck such questions.

Be that as it may, sexual activity in space has remained a completely unexplored area. In all the missions to date, astronauts have had such a heavy workload, that even if they had strong sexual cravings, they would have had neither the time nor the space for experimentation—to date, shuttles have not offered passengers private quarters for intimate activities.

Experience has shown that mixed teams work better than all-male groups during extended periods on space stations—the atmosphere is lighter.

To date there has only been one married couple in space: Mark C. Lee and N. Jan Davis on Space Shuttle Mission 47, in 1992.

Sleeping

In a weightless environment you can sleep just as well standing up as lying down. This is why the "beds" are set up in various positions around the cabin.

You will have to crawl into a fire-resistant sleeping bag with many openings so the air can circulate. Then you have to strap yourself down with three safety belts so that you won't float away during the night.

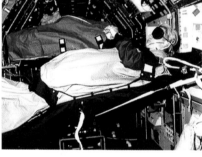

According to the *Apollo 17* astronaut Jack Schmitt, sleeping in a weightless environment is far more refreshing than sleeping on Earth. This is why, in his opinion, there were no negative after-effects when the astronauts kept waking up because of nerves, digestive problems (stomach and intestines feel very different in space), and the many unaccustomed noises in the craft—the air-conditioning and life-support systems produce a continuous wall of noise.

Medical Care

Astronauts often turn to sleeping pills. Melatonin, the sleep-inducing hormone that your body produces naturally in the evenings, is particularly popular and helpful, as there is no natural cycle of day and night in space.

You will find a very well-stocked first-aid kit on board, chock-full of every painkiller under the Sun, along with remedies for everything from motion sickness and dizziness to headaches.

One of the crew members will also be a bona fide doctor, so you can rest assured that you will be in the best of hands during the trip.

"On the back side of the Moon, on the night side, you can't see the surface. The Moon is defined simply by the absence of stars. The laws of physics tell you that your fine spacecraft is in an orbit 60 miles above it and there's no way you can hit anything. But the thought does occur, gosh, I'm skimming along just barely over the surface of a strange planet."
Michael Collins (Apollo 11)

False Color Moon: This picture, taken with numerous color filters and then reconstructed, shows the ambient factors of the lunar terrain. Mountains appear red, valleys blue to orange. Dark-blue areas, like the Mare Tranquillitatis, have more titanium than the orange areas.

Radiation Danger

The Sun is a gigantic fusion reactor in which hydrogen degrades to helium. It radiates not only visible energy but also a permanent rain of rays and particles into the universe.

Earth's magnetic field shields it from many of the rays that bombard it. This shield reaches about 60,000 kilometers (37,200 miles) into space.

In other words, this shield is still active at the altitude that space stations orbit Earth, but no longer active on the trip to the Moon or on the Moon itself. (When we fly to Mars, exposure to cosmic rays during the many years of travel might well become a major problem.)

This is why the very first experiments conducted by the pioneering Apollo crew on the Moon dealt with the effects of the profuse variety of rays.

Uncanny Sightings

All that can be said about the effect of the rays on man is that we don't know anything.

Apollo astronauts reported seeing strange flashes of light, which NASA specialists interpreted as due to the effects of cosmic rays on the optic nerve and the brain. These flashes were also seen inside the command capsule—the rays had obviously managed to penetrate the metal walls of the spacecraft.

What *is* known is that the radiation is at its most intense when sunspots are at their maximum.

These hurricanelike magnetic whirls appear on the Sun's surface about every eleven years. As a precaution, the Apollo program had scheduled its missions to the Moon during temporary periods of calm between sunspot maximums.

"Three guesses where we met!"

Restricted Visits

The uncertainty about the effects of cosmic rays on man has been one of the reasons why visits to the Moon have always been kept short.

The radiation dosage to which the Apollo crews were exposed during moon missions was 5 REM, the maximum considered allowable at the time. One REM is the natural radiation dosage one is exposed to under normal conditions on Earth.

Sun-Storm Bunkers

There is a steep rise in the intensity of the Sun's radiation during brief explosive sun storms.

During these bombarding sun-particle hurricanes, known as SEP—Solar Energetic Particle events—radioactivity can surge seventy thousand–fold.

A sophisticated SEP warning system will be a basic prerequisite before man can venture into the depths of the universe.

If man is to spend prolonged periods outside the Earth's magnetic field, SEP bunkers will have to be constructed. Spaceships that will fly to Mars will have thick-walled metal chambers or electromagnetically shielded areas to which astronauts can retire during intense sun storms.

Blueprints for accommodations on the Moon show that living quarters will be protected from constant ray bombardment by walls made of moon rock with a thickness of 1.2 to 2 meters (4 to 6 feet). The more pessimistic among the planners maintain that there will not be any

windows, and that the lunar inhabitants will have to view the surface via television monitors.

To stay within the parameters of 5 REM, extensive precautions will have to be taken during the colonization of the Moon. Work outside the moon base, for instance, will only be undertaken

The Bahamas

near an SEP bunker, and lunar workers will not be permitted to travel in a vehicle on the surface for more than 1,800 hours a year, and far less in a thin space suit.

During a sunspot minimum, radioactivity on the Moon's surface is approximately 30 REM a year. This adds up to over 1,000 REM over the period of an eleven-year sunspot cycle.

Attack on Technology

SEP storms are dangerous not only for human beings, but also for electronic equipment. It is possible to shield the equipment to some extent, but a single ionized particle landing on a microchip is enough to cause what is known as a *soft upset*—

the partial eradication of stored data. If, for instance, the navigation systems of a spacecraft were to be affected this way, there could be dire consequences, such as a sudden ignition of the engines.

A NASA report came to the conclusion that it is impossible to completely shield equipment in space from SEP storms. In other words, despite the many mishaps, the Apollo missions were basically lucky, as a NASA technician put it.

For this reason alone, your stay on the Moon might well have to be a short one. The various lunar sojourns under consideration range from six to twelve days— which, as it is, is far longer than all the Apollo missions put together.

On the Scene

Lunar Space Station

The Apollo flights circled the Moon in an elliptic orbit, ranging from 14 to 72 kilometers (8.68 to 44.64 miles) above the surface. The astronaut James Irwin reported that at the lowest orbiting altitude it felt as if they were about to crash into crater mountains.

The lunar space station orbiting the Moon will be positioned relatively near the surface, so that lunar shuttle flights can be launched as easily as possible.

As the lunar space station comes into sight, you will realize that because of its closeness to the Moon's surface, docking will have to be executed with the utmost speed. Specialized radar equipment will facilitate an automated approach and linkage, but the procedure will be a complex and risky navigational feat.

In the meantime, you will all have put on your pressure suits—no easy task in the cramped cabin. This will be a social event, for you will have to help each other. Each of you will also have to don a urine bag as discreetly as possible—with the sudden onset of gravity on the Moon, your bladder might well experience some trouble readjusting.

Wearing space suits is a prerequisite for all docking procedures, since there is a danger that one of the two capsules might depressurize. Long hoses will keep you supplied with oxygen, but in case of an emergency your space suit also has a small oxygen tank.

After docking successfully, you can disconnect the hose and remove your helmet, an irksome and time-consuming procedure that astronauts detest.

In Transit to the Moon

The lunar space station is much smaller and simpler than the big space station above Earth. Your lunar transfer vehicle will remain docked for the next few hours, for there will have to be a number of flights from the station to the Moon's surface in order for all the

Famous First Words on the Moon

"That's one small step for man; one giant leap for mankind."
Neil Armstrong (Apollo 11)

"Whoopee! Man, that may have been a small one for Neil, but that's a long one for me."
Pete Conrad (Apollo 12)

"As I stand here at Mount Hadley in the wonders of the unknown . . . I sort of realize there is a fundamental truth of our nature. Man must explore and this is exploration at its greatest."
David R. Scott (Apollo 15)

—"Okay, you're ready to go out and play in the snow?"
—"Yeah, it looks like my snowsuit's ready."
Shepard and Mitchell (Apollo 14)

passengers and equipment to be transported.

There will also be passengers returning from the Moon, and there will be lively exchanges between arriving and departing tourists, with souvenirs shown and heaps of advice offered. But some returning passengers might well come across as a little drawn. The sudden onset of weightlessness does not agree with everybody.

At last you too can climb through the hatch into the lunar lander, a spider-legged contraption that has obviously been designed for practicality. It has tiny windows and its seats are uncomfortable, but it's good enough for the short trip.

Landing on the Moon

The braking ignition of the lander's engine, slowing it down from five times the speed of sound to the mellow speed of a helicopter, lasts for about twelve minutes. The lander tilts, and you immediately feel the onset of the Moon's gravity.

The landing, too, is much like a helicopter landing. About 50 meters (164 feet) above the Moon the engine whips up a gigantic dust cloud, and then the lander steers somewhat haltingly toward the surface.

But the lunar lander's spider legs make for a soft landing, and after a featherlight touchdown, the passengers will undoubtedly start cheering.

You've made it!

Apollo Command Capsule above the Moon

On the Moon!

Each passenger in the lunar lander has a large backpack: a Personal Life Support System (PLSS), your life insurance for stepping out onto the Moon. Now a series of hoses have to be secured, for you will need more than just oxygen and pressure. There is also a well-protected hose that delivers cooling liquid for the insulation layer of your space suit and a hose with your communication cable.

Sealing your gloves and your visor is also of critical importance. Even thicker moon boots have to be slipped over the thick feet of your pressure suit, procedures you will have rehearsed many times on Earth, although things will be different in the lander's cramped quarters.

Everyone has to undergo a final seal test, and then, after a double check, the captain depressurizes the cabin.

Then he opens the hatch and is the first to climb out. So that there are no ill-feelings among the passengers, the disembarking sequence is strictly set: the oldest passenger first, followed by the second oldest, all the way down to the youngest.

As you take your first step onto the Moon, you might well remember Neil Armstrong's words. You might want to give your own first words a bit of thought: Your first steps will be caught on camera and your statement recorded!

Tips for the First Day

The first thing the pioneers did after landing was—eat. The initial plan had even been that Aldrin and Armstrong should take a five-hour nap after all the excitement of landing—a typical paper-pusher's idea. Who could take a nap at such a historic point in time! Instead, the astronauts decided to prepare themselves for the first moon walk. It took them over six hours.

Later astronauts opted for a compromise. After landing, they hooked up their pressure suits to the on-board life support system, depressurized the cabin, and opened the hatch to take a look at the lunar panorama.

Then they did go to sleep, and it was only on the following (Earth) day that they set off on their moon walk with all its complex preparations, such as setting up their PLSS, cameras, etc.

Take a lesson from the pioneers and have a nap after your first steps from the lunar lander to the moon base.

Many of the twelve pioneering astronauts on the Moon report that they slept extremely well during their first night there. After

> "I didn't mind being in that corner of the universe alone by myself. I wish someone would have communicated with me, but no one did."
> *Michael Collins* (Apollo 11)

Edwin Aldrin, the second man on the Moon

three or more restless nights spent in weightlessness, the light gravitational pull of the Moon is a very pleasant change.

You will sleep on beds with surprisingly thin mattresses, but you too will feel light as a feather. The noise of the life-support systems in the cramped spaceships is a good deal louder than those in the moon base, and the unique magic of the place will have an immediate effect on your body.

As soon as you have climbed out of your claustrophobic space suit, slipped off the irksome urine pouch, and are out of your elastic fiber-free clothes, you will undoubtedly fall into bed happy, exhausted, and strangely buoyant.

Moon Day, Moon Night

Since the Moon has no atmosphere, there is no dawn or dusk. Both moon days and moon nights last exactly fourteen Earth days, eighteen hours, twenty-two minutes, and two seconds.

It has been suggested that moon bases have clocks that indicate the Earth days, hours, and minutes that have passed since the lunar sunrise.

Earth Clock

Viewed from the Moon, Earth is constantly in the same spot in the firmament and serves as an ever-visible clock, its phases indicating periods of the moon day or moon night.

A "new Earth" indicates mid-day for the center of the visible moon side (example, at the Regiomontanus Crater), and a crescent Earth, evening. "Full Earth" indicates midnight—then the Sun is right behind you on the Moon, frontally illuminating Earth as it floats right before you. The waning Earth is the first, long-awaited sign that the lunar morning is approaching.

A "new Earth," astronauts report, is an oppressive sight. Even the most densely populated areas are steeped in darkness. There is no halo, even when the Sun shines upon Earth's atmosphere from behind; and although flashes of lightning provide a dramatic view during Earth orbits, these cannot be seen from the Moon. So the fully darkened Earth can only be pinpointed on the

lunar sky by the lack of stars in that spot.

The Terminator

The Terminator is the sharp borderline between moon night and moon day. The difference in temperature of these two zones is around 300°C (572°F), a major challenge for the designers of space suits.

> "I felt like I was an alien as I traveled through space. When I got on the Moon, I felt at home. We had mountains on three sides and had the deep canyon to the west, a beautiful spot to camp. I felt in a way as Adam and Eve must have felt, as they were standing on the Earth and they realized that they were all alone. I talk about the Moon as being a very holy place."
> *James Irwin* (Apollo 15)

James Irwin *(Apollo 15)* by Mount Hadley

You will have to come to grips with the fact that tours into the ice-cold darkness of the lunar night are pointless.

In the middle of the lunar night, Earth, fully illuminated by the Sun, bathes the Moon in faint rays. Astronauts have compared the effect to a moonlit night on Earth. But even if, from a purely mathematical standpoint, the light of a full Earth should be stronger than that of a full Moon, it will still not suffice for sightseeing or impressive lunar-landscape photos.

For this reason, trips to the Moon will be planned so that your stay will coincide mainly with lunar daytime. In the lunar night, however, you will have a much better view of the stars.

Life on the Moon Base

In the scenarios for moon tourism the concept of a "Moon Hilton" and other such fantasies keep cropping up. But do not expect too much. Basically you are a guest at a research station. The Lunar Hilton will be opening later (see page 46).

Model of a moon base

Every article on the base is of incredible value—think of the transportation costs alone. Expect flimsy disposable bedclothes, Spartan cuisine, and practically no service worth mentioning. Bona fide room service and housekeeping would make lunar hotel prices skyrocket.

Everyone working at the moon base will have a multitude of duties. A geologist might also be the doctor, and there might well be a rotation of kitchen shifts.

Care Packages for Lunar Personnel

The Artemis Project has proposed that visitors to the Moon have a "mentor" among the lunar personnel. Prior to traveling, visitors would be in radio contact with their mentors, who might ask them to run small terrestrial errands for them, and maybe even request a care package from home. Both parties benefit from this: You have a friend on the Moon with whom you've already been in phone contact, and mentors have people they can talk to in their spare time. But here, too, don't expect too much. Life on the Moon can have a profound effect on a person. And, as it is, much of the lunar personnel is likely to be made up of highly eccentric scientists. Most of them will stay for about a year at this lonely outpost, and in some cases much longer.

Spring break on the Moon

Fitness and Sports

The Moon's lower gravity will open up a whole slew of new athletic options for you. This has excited the sporting imagination of astronauts since the earliest days of space travel.

Golf

Alan Shepard was the undisputed pioneer of lunar golf. (Besides being the first American in space, he also flew to the Moon with *Apollo 14*.)

Having put in a full day's work on the Moon, he pulled a couple of golf balls out of his space suit pocket. In lieu of a club, he used the handle of his Contingency Sample Return Container, and, as he couldn't bring his hands together because of the rigidity of his space suit, he tried a one-handed swing.

His first swing missed the ball; the second grazed it, but the third was a perfect hit. Shepard radioed back the words now famous in golfing circles: "There it goes for miles and miles and miles!" (According to his *Apollo 14* colleague Mitchell, the first ball only went about 200 meters [220 yards], and the second about 360 [396 yards]). Shepard left the golf balls lying in the moon dust for "future golfers" to find.

Hiking

Mitchell and Shepard also hold the world record for the longest hike on the Moon—the crews that came after them traveled in lunar rovers.

The two astronauts went on a hike that lasted four hours and fifty minutes. They climbed the ridge of the Cone Crater, pushing a high-tech wheelbarrow in front of them through the moon dust. Shepard had to stop to rest because his heartrate had risen to over 140 and his space suit was feeling uncomfortably tight around his hips.

Soon both astronauts were pushing the wheelbarrow together, with Shepard giving the marching orders: "left, right, left, right!"

Despite the lower gravity, climbing in a space suit turned out to be much more strenuous than the control center had predicted. On the way back, the two exhausted astronauts uttered a few curses, even though NASA frowns upon the use of expletives over its airwaves. Throwing caution to the wind, Shepard uttered a hardy "Son of a bitch!"

There is a famous picture of Mitchell reading a moon map during this hike. It has gone down in history as the first picture of a moon tourist.

Track and Field

James Irwin of *Apollo 15* reports how he had finished all his tasks fifteen minutes early, and so had some "vacation time" on the Moon. He used these fifteen minutes to trot around the lunar module executing long jumps.

Despite his bulky space suit, he managed to jump 3 meters (9.9 feet) at a height of 1 meter (3.3 feet).

Setting up low-gravity Olympics on the Moon could be quite a sensation with TV viewers back home. But that would mean building stadiums with complex oxygen and life-support systems. And athletics in space suits would be too confining.

Dancing

We now know that the first men on the Moon refrained from carrying out some of the planned experiments in order to complete their mission faster and without hitches. The main emphasis was on the "show" that the world was following on TV with bated breath.

One of the end results was the "moon hop." The astronauts, people on Earth noticed, had a strange kangaroolike way of walking caused by the limiting rigidity of their space suits and the Moon's lower gravity. This gave rise in terrestrial dance clubs to the popular, though short-lived, moon hop.

Ever since, a couple of kangaroo hops have remained a staple of every moon walk, and you should continue the tradition.

Of all the astronauts, Jack Schmitt of *Apollo 17* was the one to alight in the most spectacular way. While gathering moon-rock

Lunar sports that didn't catch on

samples, Schmitt lost his balance, pirouetted, and landed on his hands and knees. As he got up, checking his camera to see if it was still working, his colleague, Parker, told him that the switchboard was already "lit up by calls from the Houston Ballet Foundation," requesting his services for the next season.

Schmitt went ahead and auditioned then and there, becoming the first astronaut to truly test the limits of a space suit. His leg high up in the air, he executed two spectacular classical jumps.

The crater where this performance took place has gone down in history as "The Ballet Crater."

Dancing in a low-gravity environment can be a rewarding experience, but keep to the moon base. Jumping and twirling in a space suit on the lunar surface can be both uncomfortable and dangerous.

Games

Dave Scott of *Apollo 15* surprised television viewers throughout the world with the famous feather experiment, proving Galileo's theory that in a vacuum all objects fall at the same speed.

Scott had secretly plucked a feather from the falcon mascot of the Air Force Academy, and now, standing on the edge of the Hadley Rille, held it next to a heavy geological hammer. He let go of both objects at the same time, and millions of viewers watched them drift down side by side, landing together after a 1.3 second fall.

Unfortunately, his colleague James Irwin stepped on the feather, and it could no longer be found in the moon dust. A priceless trophy for later souvenir hunters— providing that anyone can get away with digging around at the sacred Apollo landing sites, which have already been declared Historical Lunar Monuments.

Souvenirs

"Don't forget to bring me something nice!" These parting words that every traveler hears time and again take on a new meaning when your destination is the Moon. In lunar travel there is also the reverse tradition of taking something terrestrial up to the Moon. From the pioneering Apollo days, teddy bears or wedding rings that have lain in the moon dust have turned into cherished mementos for the astronauts.

Rocks

Needless to say, the number one lunar souvenir is a chunk of the Moon—and lucky for you, the whole place is littered with rocks of every size.

The first Apollo crews gathered up pretty much any rock that seemed halfway unusual, carting back 382 kilograms (842 pounds). Jack Schmitt of *Apollo 17,* a professional geologist, was somewhat disappointed at how similar all the rocks looked and would have liked to dig much deeper than had been scheduled for his moon walk.

Geologists have classified the lunar surface as regolith. What you mainly will find there is moon dust, which includes particles under 1 centimeter in diameter (you can store it in an empty film roll), and crystalline clumps of magma.

Moon rock belongs to the basalt family and was formed by a melting-down process. The Moon's magma was runnier than the magma from terrestrial volcanoes, and as a result moon rocks are not very solid in structure.

There are often miniscule craters on moon rocks, which are the result of bombardment by micrometeorites. Sometimes these minicraters have little mounds in their center, just as the large craters do.

Meteor impacts released so much energy that the center of these minicraters was melted down into all kinds of bulb-shaped and cylindrical crystal particles.

"I don't want just any old moon rock! I want something special!"

The resulting bright beads are usually only a few tenths of a millimeter wide. But with some patience and a little luck you can extract some exceptional gems.

Some moon rocks have hollow ducts inside that were formed when gasses escaped as the magma cooled. While you are out gathering rocks, remember the official weight limit: Whatever the rocks weigh on the Moon, multiply that by six!

The chemical constitution of moon rock is silicon, aluminum, iron, calcium, manganese, magnesium, sulfur, cobalt, titanium, and nickel. It is the high titanium content that is responsible for the rock's dark color.

On the Moon there are no precious metals or valuable ores that could make you rich over night. You will have to make do with the moon rocks' spiritual value and the adventure of obtaining them.

Special Treasures

Scott and Irwin of *Apollo 15* took the first U.S. postage stamps into space—the famous commemorative series "United States in Space, a decade of achievement."

"To show that our good Postal Service has deliveries any place in the universe," Scott announced with a flourish, "I have the pleasant task of canceling, here on the Moon, the first stamp of a new issue dedicated to commemorate United States achievements in space." And, standing at the edge of the Hadley Rille, he stamped the envelope with a custom-made stamp with the first-edition date, August 2, 1971.

All six Apollo lunar modules, after having lifted off from the Moon and docked with their command modules, were left to crash on the Moon at a precisely calculated spot.

The widespread fragments from these wrecks will make prime souvenirs. It would be a good idea, however, to take some shovels along with you, as much of the wreckage will be buried deep in the moon dust.

The wreckage of *Apollo 15* will be by far the most interesting find. In their hasty transfer to the command module, Scott and Irwin forgot to take their pilot boxes with them.

These boxes were full of mementos, ennobled by having been on the Moon: flags, gold coins, medals, letters, and even some plastic shamrocks that James Irwin, an Irishman born on St. Patrick's Day, had taken along.

But the single most important item in these lost pilot boxes was the commemorative day-of-issue envelope—for philatelists, the holy grail.

Other priceless moon souvenirs of terrestrial provenance are the remains of the Russian space probes. The first pile of Earth wreckage to hit the Moon was *Luna 2,* which crashed on November 13, 1959. It is thought to be lying somewhere near the Mare Imbrium, between Archimedes and Autolycus, in a private crater it made upon impact.

A particularly hot item would be a piece of wreckage from one of the secret Soviet probes. In 1965, during the height of the lunar race, the Soviet Union launched six Luna probes, of which only four flew in the right direction. Of these, one flew right past the Moon, and the remaining three landed with a thud.

But don't set your hopes too high. If, for instance, you were to fly over the Sahara, you'd have a hard enough time pinpointing an object the size of a car, and on camelback, your chances would be practically nil. The near side of the Moon is almost three times the size of the Sahara, with many more gorges and ravines.

Prospects

Mining the Moon

"Is the surface of the Earth really the right place for an expanding technological civilization?" Gerard K. O'Neill, the president of the Space Studies Institute, asks. According to him, there is enough oxygen, silicon, metal ore, and other raw materials on the Moon to set up an independent mining concern.

The limitless supply of solar energy could also be harnessed to create fuel and propellants, turning the Moon into an economically feasible launch pad for traveling deep into space.

According to O'Neill, the gigantic empty hydrogen tanks of the space shuttles could also be put to good use on the Moon. Instead of jettisoning them into the oceans, the tanks could be cost-effectively towed to the Moon and used either as building material for the moon bases, or as holding tanks for fuel produced on the Moon.

There are quite a few high-flying plans for unmanned prospecting robots that could go poking around the Moon looking for mineral treasures.

The highest hopes are set on the meteorite ice of the Moon's south pole. This could provide the foundation for the production of . . .

Lunar Energy

For billions of years, moon dust has been bombarded with energy-rich cosmic rays, creating rare inert gasses. While analyzing

Controlled Ecological Life Support System (CELSS): Plants supply oxygen and food

lunar samples for materials that do not exist on Earth, scientists came upon the inert gas isotope, helium 3.

Combined with water, helium 3 could be turned into an ideal fuel for the fusion reactor that is currently being developed. Through opencast mining, specialized robots could heat up and distill moon dust to create helium 3.

Not an easy task, though. An 18-ton "mobile miner" that can plow through 1,300 tons of moon dust an hour, could produce 33 kilograms (72.75 pounds) of helium 3 a year. In other words, a whole army of mobile miners would be needed to produce the 5 tons of helium 3 needed to supply the United States with a year's worth of energy.

Unmanned rockets could then transport the helium 3 back to Earth. The energy output of this futuristic fuel is incredible. Even if one ton of helium 3 were to cost a billion dollars, it would still be the equivalent of buying gas at only $7 a barrel.

There is definitely enough helium 3 lying around on the Moon just waiting to be mined. Scientists estimate that there is ten times more energy to be harnessed from helium 3 than from all the oil, gas, and coal resources on Earth.

Japanese Moon Cities

Obayashi Enterprises in Japan is the worldwide leader in the blueprints for colonizing the Moon. Obayashi has concrete visions of a gigantic biosphere in which bacteria provide clean air and plant cultures sufficient for nutrition. There will be mechanisms to absorb meteorites. The building of a tourist rocket, Kankoh Maru, is next on the agenda.

After 2007 the multiple-use rocket, which has already been introduced to the public, is scheduled to begin taking fifty passengers on day trips into space. The projected ticket price is $15,000. In a later phase, Kankoh Maru will head on to the space stations, and even later, to the lunar cities. The Japanese Rocket Society, a union of various space-travel firms, can expect a sum of $20 billion in government subventions for the development of its projects. Market research has already been conducted: Seventy percent of the Japanese would be prepared to pay an equivalent of up to three months wages for a trip into space. It is estimated that in 2025 a two-week trip to the Moon should come to about $50,000.

The Japanese do not lack self-confidence. Takao Saito of Obayashi Enterprises says that the Moon is just a test: Their real goal is Mars.

The Straits of Mozambique

Excursions

Means of Transport

How are you going to get about on the Moon? The question is trickier than you might think. You won't get very far on foot in your cumbersome space suit and with your limited oxygen supply. Moon walking will never catch on as a sport.

Electrocars, moon rovers, or the larger and hardier lunar vehicles of the future will do much to widen your range.

But here, too, there will be limits to where you can go. The lunar terrain is incredibly rugged and covered with jagged rocks, and deadly crevices and fissures lie hidden beneath the moon dust.

On the relatively flat lunar oceans you can travel at a maximum of 30 kilometers per hour (18.6 miles per hour), but every couple of kilometers you will run into craters and crevices. A thorough overland exploration of the Moon seems impossible anytime soon. There are dreamers who envision monorail trains and cable cars taking tourists to points of interest. But how would all the building material be transported to the Moon? These would be investments without a yield.

The Moon Buggy

The chances that the moon buggies left by the Apollo missions might still be functioning after all these years are relatively low. These vehicles, officially known as LRVs (lunar roving vehicles), weighed 270 kilograms (595 pounds) on Earth and could reach a speed of up to 18 kilometers per hour (11 miles per hour). They were used by *Apollos 15, 16,* and *17,* and together covered a distance of 36 kilometers (22.32 miles) on the Moon in four and a half hours.

The two 36-volt silver-and-zinc batteries will have given up the ghost by now. They were built to work at temperatures ranging from 4°C to 52°C (39.2°F to 125.6°F), and the astronauts had to constantly administer cooling agents and heat shields after every use.

"You see? This is what I hate about these tours!"

The manufacturer of the buggies, GM Delco, maintains that the LRV should still be in fine working condition, "as long as you take a couple of new batteries along." But according to Saverio Morea of the NASA Marshall Space Flight Center in Alabama, it is uncertain whether the delicate vehicle will have withstood the countless temperature cycles since the last Apollo crew left the Moon.

Members of the American Moon Tourism Association have pledged to fence in the landing sites of the pioneering Apollo missions and to preserve them as historic sites for future generations.

Spider-Legged Rockets

Since there is no atmosphere on the Moon, it is impossible to fly; rockets are the only option. There are many plans for lunar modules in the works, similar in concept to the LTV (lunar transfer vehicle), spider-legged capsules powered by rocket drives. After a powerful blastoff, they shoot like missiles on a 45-degree trajectory above the surface, and then, as they come in for a landing, a second blast from their jets slows them down.

Steering these ballistic vehicles is extremely difficult, as astronauts found out during the early Apollo training sessions. To practice landing on the Moon, they had a "flying bedstead," which gave them a run for their money. On three occasions the astronauts had to bail out of the craft at the very last moment. The problem was that the instant the craft ventured out of its flight path, it was impossible to maneuver it back with its one rocket jet.

In our recommendations of various points of interest in this chapter, we are presupposing that a reliable transport system has been set up.

Alone on the Moon

For your own safety, it is unlikely you will be permitted to hike around on the Moon on your own. But if you would like to go on a short, unsupervised moon walk, you will have to sign up for a special course at the training camp, which will familiarize you with the technicalities of your space suit's life-support system, and be given a high-tech emergency device. The instant your breathing becomes irregular, an alarm goes off.

Don't wander too far from the moon base. You can experience the full effect of the Moon once all traces of civilization disappear behind the first ridge.

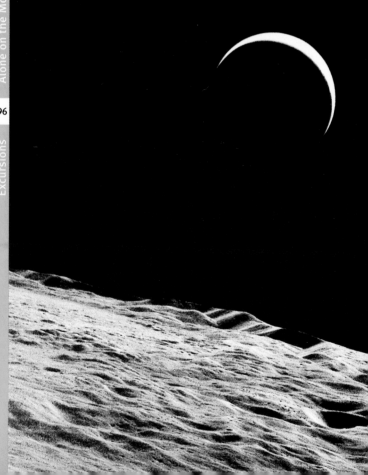

Every moon traveler has been profoundly moved by the view of Earth in the distance. Prepare yourself for a rush of contradictory emotions, ranging from extreme loneliness to glowing love for your home planet.

To date no research has been conducted on the psychological and spiritual effects of leaving Earth's gravitational and magnetic fields with their manifold energies.

People in space stations orbiting Earth are still within its sphere of influence. But on the Moon you enter a completely new realm of experience.

Some specialists believe that a trip to the Moon can be medically beneficial for certain psychological dysfunctions. NASA's Jesco von Puttkamer speaks of the "overview effect." An overbearing ego, facing the vastness of the

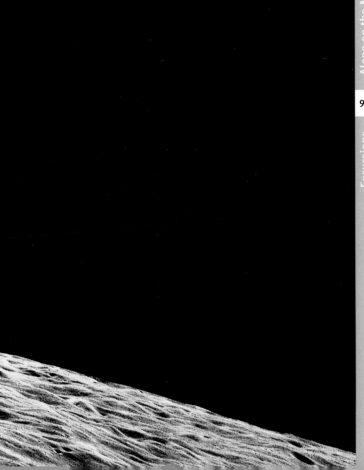

universe, could find its proper dimensions.

Besides the many scientific benefits of exploring the Moon, there are also parascientific and spiritual benefits.

The first moon travelers reported that their steps and leaps on the Moon have remained deeply embedded in their memory. Some of them exercised secret rituals that they have never spoken about. Between them and the Moon there is a covert bond.

The lunar environment, so alien to man, opens up new regions in his consciousness, affording a clearer view not only of the universe, but also of the inner workings of the psyche. As man travels to the Moon, he travels with the beliefs he brings from Earth. Most of the American astronauts have been devout Christians who brought with them their faith and convictions. When man finds himself in extreme circumstances, his faith is truly put to the test. In the light of the Moon it is clear what your true convictions are.

As you travel to the Moon, there will be much to-do about science, physics, and technology. But don't let this disturb your focus on yourself and your experiences.

You must also face your fear and not try to deal with it through planning and training.

A large dose of pioneer spirit and basic beliefs are the best ways of dealing with unexpected situations.

"The Earth would eventually be so small I could blot it out of the universe simply by holding up my thumb."
Buzz Aldrin (Apollo 11)

Buzz Aldrin, photographed by
Neil Armstrong *(Apollo 11)*

Excursions on the Bright Side

The Best Time of the Day

Note that the best time for tours is the early moon morning. Then the stones are still cool and the temperatures bearable.

It is also the best time for photographing, as the light coming from the side beautifully brings out the structures of the Moon's surface.

In order to make planning easier for you, the time of sunrise at your excursion's goal is indicated, for the sake of simplicity, in the classic form: time (in Earth days) from the new Moon, first quarter, half Moon, last quarter, or full Moon. At the beginning of each paragraph, you will find the approximate coordinates of the location so you can find the place in a moon atlas.

The Schröter Valley

Location: 26° N, 51° W
Sunrise four days after the first quarter

It is already clear through a moderately good telescope from Earth that this valley has something special about it. Vallis Schröteri is in total 160 kilometers (99.2 miles) long and begins 25 kilometers (15.5 miles) north of the Crater Herodotus with a peculiar formation, which, from above, resembles the head of a cobra.

A hike of several kilometers in a space suit makes little sense, so you should choose as your starting point the sharp curve west of the Crater Freud.

Here the valley has a depth of more than 1,000 meters (1,100 yards) and is barely 500 meters (1,650 feet) across—in other words, a more impressive scale than that of the Grand Canyon on Earth.

The more daring will let themselves down here by means of the moon rover's winch, but the most beautiful view is from above. You can see deep into the canyon to the left and right; its bottom is illuminated only when the Sun is in a favorable spot.

A wavy channel winds along the bottom of the valley, giving the

Vallis Schröteri

impression that earlier a river must have dug its course into the stone. But, as always, it is left over from once-seething lava.

The Straight Wall
Location: 22° S, 8° W
Sunrise not quite a day after the first quarter

An impressive landscape awaits the moon visitor near the Crater Birt in the Mare Nubium. The Rupes Recta, the "Straight Wall," is also clearly visible from Earth with a smallish telescope.

The fault, over 100 kilometers (62 miles) long and 240 meters (792 feet) high, between two basalt plains, forms a smooth, 40-degree slope. It is a fantastic natural drama.

Because of the short distance to the horizon on the Moon, it appears as if the decline between the upper and the lower plain goes on forever and reaches around the entire Moon. The effect is best appreciated from the upper plain, which is why this point belongs to the fixed itinerary of every tour.

Materials on the Moon Floor
Location: 8° N, 59° W
Sunrise five days after the first quarter

West of the Crater Reiner, in the Oceanus Procellarum, the moon floor shows peculiar discolorations that resemble a fish with a frayed fantail.

Detail photographs from on board the lunar probes *Lunar Orbiter* and *Clementine* show no relief features whatsoever.

So this structure, called the Reiner Gamma, must consist of odd irregularities in the otherwise uniformly colored dust that covers the Moon. Japanese mining firms hope that these might be exposed layers that would be worth mining.

"Instead of an intellectual search, there was suddenly a very deep gut feeling that something was different. It occurred when looking at Earth and seeing this blue-and-white planet floating there.
Edgar Mitchell (Apollo 14)

The Alps
Location: 45° N, 0°
Sunrise shortly before the first
quarter

Here you can yodel. Yes, there really are alps on the Moon. The mighty Montes Alpes lie a little farther north than do those on Earth; they stretch a good 250 kilometers (155 miles) east from the easily visible Crater Plato.

As on Earth, there are impressive mountains here, up to 2,400 meters (7,920 feet) high.

From the surface, they present a bizarre scene. Toward the south the Moon Alps suddenly cease, and Cape Agassiz plunges like a steep sea cliff into the Mare Imbrium.

True to form, the Cape was named for a Swiss naturalist. A good 50 kilometers (31 miles) to the north rises the mighty Mons Blanc, although its 3,600 meter (11,880 feet) height is more than a kilometer lower than its earthly counterpart's. On its eastern rim lies one of the best-known valleys on the Moon, the 180-kilometer-long (111.6 miles) Vallis Alpes.

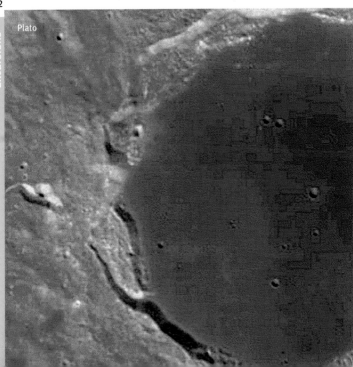

Plato

The valley floor is smooth, indicating that it was flooded during the phase of liquid moon rocks.

A very narrow, twisting channel goes down the middle of the valley. In the west of the valley there are magnificent views of the alpine peaks, which here rise up especially high and in odd formations.

Seen from Earth, the Moon Alps offer dramatic images at sunrise, when long, pointed shadows give the impression of steeply rising columns.

Vallis Alpes

Moon Caves
Location: 0°, 24° E
Sunrise five days after the new Moon

On Earth, lava forms many kinds of chambers and pipes, and on the Moon, too, people have long suspected that there are underground cavities. The relatively short Apollo missions could not turn up any such formations, but only 45 kilometers (27.9 miles) south of the *Apollo 11* landing site there is a location with remarkable lava formations.

The Crater Moltke is perfectly round, 7 kilometers (4.34 miles) in diameter, and 1,300 meters (4,290 feet) deep. Because of that, even in the middle of the crater floor you have the surrounding mountains in view. You have to get over the sharp rim of the crater on foot.

The ideal time to be at this point would be one day after sunrise, so that the Terminator (the sharp borderline between moon night and moon day) would be in the middle of the crater.

There must have been many lava pipes in and around Moltke, which have in the meantime partly collapsed and left behind caves in all sorts of sizes. But be careful exploring on your own: The stone is extremely crumbly, indicating that any cave is in great danger of collapsing.

For settlement on the Moon, such possibilities for underground storage are important, since equipment can be stored there at fairly constant temperatures.

Descartes

Location: 9° S, 0°

Sunrise one day before the first quarter

This area, strewn with numerous decayed craters, is where *Apollo 16* landed, 50 kilometers (31 miles) north of Descartes and 60 kilometers (37.2 miles) west of Zöllner.

Apollo 16 landing site

At that time, to go on an excursion with the lunar rover south of the landing site was of special interest to geologists. A chain of five craters, given the working name "Cinco" (Spanish for "five") by NASA, promised to be of volcanic origin.

On the scene the astronauts quickly determined that there were no traces of volcanoes.

On the basis of their geologic training, they immediately saw from the lunar fragments that, like all the rest, they had originated from meteorite impacts.

"Tom is totally out of it! He's been mooning about all day!"

Mad Channels

Location: 8° N, 6° E
Sunrise not quite one day before
the first quarter

Crazy formations in a crazy region:
The entire area between Mare
Vaporum, Sinus Medii, and Mare
Tranquillitatis is full of fissured
structures radiating out from
decayed craters as if a huge storm
had blown over them.

In the plain north of the Crater
Agrippa lie several large channels.
Among them the Rima Hyginus is
striking in that it divides the Crater
Hyginus through the middle.
Farther to the northwest, this
channel, several hundred meters
in depth, transforms itself into a
series of crater ditches that are
connected with each other. With a
good lunar rover, this channel
offers good prospects for future
off-road fun.

The best-known and most var-
ied channel system on the Moon
begins southwest of Hyginus,
around the 2,760-meter-high
(9,108 feet) Crater Triesnecker.
The channels, most 1 to 2 kilometers (.62 to 1.24 miles) across,
seem from Earth to be bottomless
fissures on account of their steep
walls.

Because the channels continually branch off, there had been
repeated speculation that they
were a road system built by moon
inhabitants.

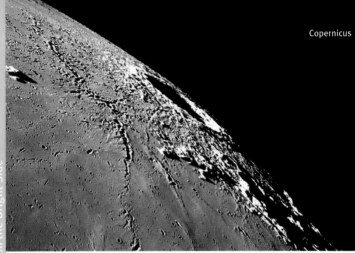

Round about Copernicus

Location: 10° N, 20° W

One and a half days after the first quarter

The dominant feature of the bright side of the Moon is the colossal Crater Copernicus, a furrowed circular mountain 93 kilometers (57.66 miles) in diameter, whose floor lies 3,760 meters (12,408 feet) deeper than the wall surrounding it. The outside of the crater is totally impassable, rising up to 900 meters (2,970 feet) above the surrounding region. The chances are poor for ever reaching on foot the imposing central mountains, up to 1,200 meters (3,960 feet) high, inside the crater. But Copernicus will be a favorite goal of lunar tourist flights.

Don't miss the double-crater Fauth, some 12 kilometers (7.44 miles) across, 50 kilometers (31 miles) south of the south rim of Copernicus, that has the shape of a keyhole. It is an important orientation point for moon flyers.

Copernicus

Epsilon Peak

Location: 90° S, 0°

The south pole offers visitors friendly temperature zones wherever the Sun is.

The highest mountain range on the Moon is the Leibnitz Range, near the South Pole. The peaks of the crater rims rise over 10,000 meters (33,000 feet) above the surrounding terrain, higher than the highest mountains on Earth.

This region had become known only since the opening up of the Moon because the South Pole is hard to see from Earth and cannot be explored satisfactorily by lunar probes.

The popular French astronomer Camille Flammarion (1842–1925) called Epsilon Peak, 9,050 meters (29,865 feet) high, the "mountain of eternal light" because some part of it is always illuminated by the Sun, whatever the phase of the Moon may be. The peak seems to glow in all the colors of the rainbow, so that in the nineteenth century people thought it was covered with snow. Amundsen Plain, at the foot of Epsilon Peak, however, remains in eternal darkness, which is why great hopes are directed at this part of the Moon.

The Moon's poles have become a special attraction, thanks to the discovery in 1998 of the presence of water. The remains of innumerable icy comets have been preserved in the eternal shadow of the crater rims near the poles. This ice can lie up to 3 meters (10 feet) beneath the lunar surface.

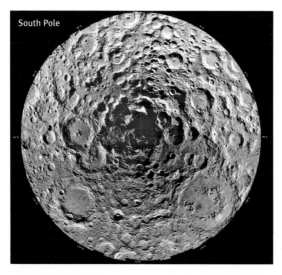

South Pole

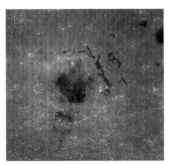

Mons Gruithuisen Gamma

Hortensius

Mons Gruithuisen Gamma
Location: 36° N, 40° W
Sunrise three days after the first quarter

This circular mountain mass, 20 kilometers (12.4 miles) wide, is a strange sight to see. The smooth mountaintop looks like collapsed pudding; it is apparently the result of a giant gas bubble in the underlying rock.

On the peak, a small, smooth crater rises saucily, 900 meters (2,970 feet) across—a popular test for astronomers with bigger telescopes.

Directly across in a westerly direction lies Gruithuisen Delta, which must have once looked

much like this, but is strongly weathered. One hundred kilometers (62 miles) south of both lies the crater of the same name, which looks like the pudding mold for the pudding mountain.

Dome near Hortensius
Location: 7°N, 28°W
Sunrise two and a half days after the first quarter

Still more such domes, if not quite so large (10 to 12 kilometers [6.2 to 7.44 miles] in diameter, 300 to 400 meters [990 to 1,320 feet] high) lie north of the Crater Hortensius. Oddly, they all have on their backs a small crater 1 kilometer (.62 miles) across. They might be volcanic phenomena.

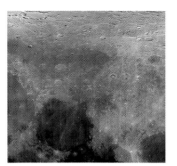
Sea of Death

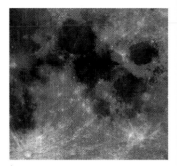
Lamont

The Sea of Death
Location: 45° N, 28° E
Sunrise two days before the first quarter

Here there was once a gigantic crater 150 kilometers (93 miles) across with steeply rising walls, which filled with liquid rock from the depths of the Moon. The wall has since weathered in a most picturesque fashion: Furrows and channels crisscross the solidified sea, and right in the middle of the circular plain is the Crater Bürg, which arose later and is 40 kilometers (24.8 miles) across.

Broad sea arms radiate to the north and southwest of it, as if giant arms from the bottom of the sea were about to push the bothersome crater away.

The Spirits Crater
Location: 5° N, 23° E
Sunrise two days before the first quarter

Lamont is unique. It is a crater 75 kilometers (46.5 miles) across, that is in reality not a crater at all, but was formed from sea ridges in the western part of the Mare Tranquillitatis. These ridges, which arose during the Storm and Stress period of lunar geologic history through uprising magma, are up to 10 kilometers (6.2 miles) across and up to 200 meters (660 feet) high.

Flying over them, they appear like the shallow chains of hills in the foothills of the Alps, stretching over many hundreds of kilometers to the north of the landing site of the first men on the Moon.

Tycho

Tycho
Location: 43° S, 11° W
Sunrise one day after the first quarter

Tycho, about 100 million years old, is one of the youngest craters, as one can easily determine from Earth. Its system of rays made up of ejected material stretches over 1,500 kilometers (930 miles) and covers all older craters.

At full Moon, Tycho (near the South Pole) is the Moon's most striking feature. The bright crater floor is surrounded by a dark ring about 150 kilometers (93 miles) in diameter. Next to it the gigantic field of the bright ejected material can easily be made out. The whole gives the full Moon the appearance of an orange, with Tycho as its navel. Tycho also offers visitors to the Moon a spectacular view. With a diameter

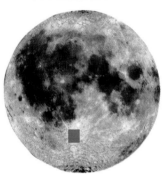

of 85 kilometers (52.7 miles) and a depth of 4,850 meters (16,005 feet), it is one of the most imposing circular mountains. The central peak in the middle of the crater is 1,600 meters (5,280 feet) high, and the very uneven ground makes exploratory trips almost impossible. But from its rim, Tycho is one of the most photogenic craters.

The Crater that Overflowed
Location: 50° S, 60° W
Sunrise two to three days before the full Moon

Normally the floor of a crater always lies lower than the surroundings. Here is the exception: After its creation, the Crater Wargentin, 84 kilometers (52.08 miles) across, was filled up to its starched collar with lava, so that it now forms a circular high surface with Y-shaped sea ridges.

The Living Puzzle

Location: 28° N, 12° E

Sunrise one day before the first quarter

The small, young Crater Linné (2.4 kilometers [1.5 miles] across, 600 meters [1,980 feet] deep) has created much excitement since the second half of the nineteenth century. The German lunar investigator Julius Schmidt (1825–84) raised the alarm in 1866. The small crater appeared to have transformed itself into a cloud, and other observers soon after made out a small depression. They thought it might be the ash cloud of a volcano or liquid lava that had filled the crater and spilled over the rim.

The American astronomer William Henry Pickering thought that the white spot was a ring of hoarfrost, which visibly shrank in the sunlight—shrank so much that several observers reported the complete disappearance of Linné.

Finally it turned out that all these observations were wrong—characteristic for observations at the outer limit of a telescope's resolution. When you visit, all that will remain of the whole flap is a neat story for the tour guide.

Rydberg

The Museum

Location: 1° N, 23° E

Sunrise two days before the first quarter

The landing site of the first manned lunar module at the edge of the Mare Tranquillitatis is a restricted zone, which is being exploited to the hilt as a goal for pilgrimage.

The site is proudly listed on moon maps as Touchdown (Statio Tranquillitatis). Neil Armstrong's first footprint from July 21, 1969, will have been long protected from destruction by a Plexiglas cover. The lower part of the lunar lander, the flag, and the instruments left behind have not been altered since that noteworthy date either.

If you stand in a fairly large group of moon visitors and listen to the impassioned words of the guide, you will not be able to escape the fascination of this place. But you can only feel what it

was like to be a pioneer if you decide to go on a tour by yourself. (See page 96.)

North of the landing site lie three small craters, which were named after the first moon explorers. Crater Armstrong to the east, 4.6 kilometers (2.9 miles) across, was called Sabine E on old moon maps. The associated main Crater Sabine, 30 kilometers (18.6 miles) in diameter, lies 150 kilometers (93 miles) to the west, and was not named after a woman, but for

the Irish astronomer Sir Edward Sabine (1788–1883).

Thirty kilometers (18.6 miles) west of Armstrong lies Crater Collins, with a diameter of only 2.4 kilometers (1.5 miles). As pilot of the lunar module, Collins did not have the chance to walk on the Moon. Crater Aldrin is 3.4 kilometers (2.1 miles) across, and, like the others, anything but exciting. Nevertheless, no tour will miss pointing them out.

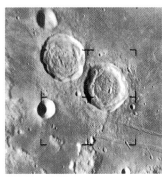

Ritter and Sabine

The Bridge

Location: 15° N, 48° E

Sunrise four days after the new Moon

On July 29, 1953, John O'Neill, science editor of the *New York Herald Tribune,* discovered, looking at the Moon with his own telescope, a most unique formation: a bridge on the western edge of the Mare Crisium that joined Cape Lavinium to Cape Olivium.

According to his calculations, the "gigantic natural bridge" had a span of 30 kilometers (18.6 miles) and a breadth of 2 kilometers (1.24 miles). The discovery created excitement in the press, especially after a UFO enthusiast maintained that spectrum photos taken by the Mount Wilson Observatory showed that the structure was made of iron.

The O'Neill Bridge would have become a first-class attraction for moon tourists, but unfortunately it turned out to be, after the photos from *Lunar Orbiter,* just another mistaken observation.

Taurus-Littrow, Mare Serenitatis. The picture shows Harrison H. Schmitt *(Apollo 17)*.

Where Gravity Is Greatest
Location: 18° N, 58° E
Sunrise two to four days after the new Moon

The Mare Crisium presents a surprisingly dark appearance. It might have been formed by a gigantic impact in the early history of the Moon. Its shape is like a crater with a diameter of 570 kilometers (353.4 miles).

If you look at the Moon from Earth, this dark oval sea is one of the most striking features. If the Moon's disk were a watch face, Mare Crisium would be precisely between two and three o'clock; in other words, on the right edge of the Moon's disk (as observed from the northern latitudes; if you are south of the equator, the Moon is "standing on its head").

The inside of the bowl was flooded by mighty layers from several lava flows. This created an excess of material that has resulted in anomalies in the Moon's gravity at this spot. As a visitor, you will probably not notice the concentration of mass ("Mascon") here, but on a scale you would weigh several hundred grams more at this place than elsewhere on the Moon.

The Russian probe *Luna 23* landed in the southern part of the Mare Crisium on October 28, 1974, and a week later returned to Earth. According to long-established space-travel custom, it left behind a lovely tablet with hammer and sickle.

The precise landing spot is still unknown, and if you discover traces of this unmanned visitor, the Russian moon experts will be glad to hear from you.

> "You look out the window and you're looking back across blackness of space a quarter of a million miles away, looking back at the most beautiful star in the heavens. The Earth is surrounded by blackness, though you're looking through sunlight. When the Sun shines through space it's black. What are you looking at? What are you looking through? You can call it the universe, but it's the infinity of space and the infinity of time."
> *Eugene Cernan* (Apollo 10, 17)

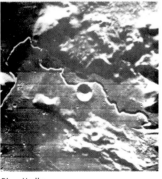

Rima Hadley

"Don't worry about overcrowding. All our executive committee and shareholder meetings will be held on the Moon."

Red Spots
Location: 21° S, 22° W
Sunrise two days after the first quarter

Another famous "bridge" spans the Bullialdus W. Valley, which stretches northwest of the majestic Crater Bullialdus in the Mare Nubium.

When the Sun is high, the low mountain ridge of the Crater Agatharchides O looks like a wide lava board spanning the 15-kilometer-wide (9.3 miles) valley in an elegant arc.

Directly west of it, it seems as if a steeper ridge also stretches across the valley. But when the Sun's position changes, it quickly becomes clear that these are nothing but raised ground with no space beneath.

Bullialdus, however, could be attractive for another reason: It belongs to the few craters in whose vicinity peculiar light phenomena

in the form of red spots have been observed, which last for only a few minutes at a time.

There are apparently in this region certain luminescent forms of rock that are stimulated by the intense ultraviolet light of the Sun to produce a "cold light." Or it is a weak sign of volcanic activity, which scientists have long hoped to glimpse.

Excursions on the Dark Side

The dark side of the Moon lacks the best that the bright side has to offer: a view of Earth. Otherwise, it holds no secrets. The landscape, seen from a great height, is totally different from that on the bright side. Maria and mountains are almost totally absent; there are a few really big craters, with extensive fields of rubble between them, with one crater next to the other.

Because of the lack of maria, the dark side is much more difficult to get around on and less interesting for opencast mining.

Why the two sides are so different is one of the many unexplained secrets of the Moon; your visit might bring the solution a little bit closer.

The dark side will only be developed for tourism later, if at all. As far as its formations are concerned, there is less variety than on the bright side, and because of scientific investigation, visitors are less welcome here than on the bright side.

The Observatory

Location: 22° S, 130° E

The most realistic among all the possibilities for using the Moon is the building of an astronomical observatory on the side facing away from Earth. It lies in the "radio shadow" of Earth, whose innumerable sources of radiation, at all possible frequencies, greatly interfere with radio astronomy. For traditional astronomic observations into the depths of space, the

"Suddenly from behind the rim of the Moon, in long, slow-motion moments of immense majesty, there emerges a sparkling blue and white jewel, a light, delicate sky-blue sphere laced with slowly swirling veils of white, rising gradually like a small pearl in a thick sea of black mystery. It takes more than a moment to fully realize this is Earth . . . home."
Edgar Mitchell (Apollo 14)

solid Moon offers a far more stable platform than the Hubbell space telescope whirling in its orbit.

Such an observatory would have to be manned constantly in order to maintain the expensive equipment. It would appear to be the most promising point for the beginning of moon tourism.

Individual groups of visitors are welcome when the observatory, in the middle of the lunar day, is in full sunlight. Then radio astronomic measurements and optical

observations are both subject to disturbance.

You will be welcomed, not least because you ensure the financing of this costly research enterprise. You will be counted on to report enthusiastically about this farthest outpost of civilization back on Earth.

The Far Side Lunar Observatory (FSLO) is a lonely, frightening place. Deep beneath the Moon's surface, well-protected from cosmic rays, are the living and working quarters of this small contingent. It is all somewhat reminiscent of the Antarctic.

A shallow secondary crater within the mighty Tsiolkovsky crater will contain the biggest radio antenna in the "world," with a diameter of 1.5 kilometers (.93 miles). Twenty-seven antennas, each 50 meters (165 feet) in diameter, arranged in the form of a gigantic Y, from a synthetic radio telescope with which scientists hope to decipher the rate of expansion of the universe.

> "You suddenly start to realize you're in deep space, that planets are just that, they're planets, and you're not really connected to anything anymore. You are floating through this deep black void."
> *Edgar Mitchell* (Apollo 14)

Another huge structure, consisting of forty telescopes in two circles, is the LOUISA (Lunar Optical Ultraviolet-Infrared Synthesis Array).

With this most powerful measuring instrument ever built, the hope is finally to be able to observe directly planets circling neighboring fixed stars.

Other instruments explore the cosmos in the X ray and many other spectrums. Because there is no distorting atmosphere, most of the equipment is simply set up on the Moon's surface.

The radio-interferometer of the FSLO is synchronized with radio telescopes in New Mexico, and thus forms an instrument 380,000 kilometers (235,600 miles) across, the

Tsiolkovsky

Moon-Earth-Radio-Interferometer (MERI), with which the most precise observations can be carried out down to a thirty-millionth second of arc.

Russia and America

Location: 40° S, 150° W
Sunrise two and a half days after the last quarter

Because it was the Russians who, with the help of the *Luna 3* probe on October 7, 1959, were able to publish the first pictures of the dark side of the Moon, many of the craters on the far side bear the names of Russian scientists.

The Russians proudly called an especially impressive formation the "Soviet Mountains" (Montes Sovietici). But later American photos showed that these Soviet "Mountains" must have been a photographic error. Nevertheless, the Russian authorities refused to remove the ominous mountain range from their moon maps.

Only in 1979 was the quarrel settled, at a meeting of the International Astronomical Union (I.A.U.). As compensation for their lost mountains, the Russians submitted a list of eight new crater names for the dark side of the Moon.

One of them, the Lipsky Crater, appeared as a beautiful round crater in the Russian moon atlas. But at this spot the American maps again showed nothing. To keep the matter from escalating, the clever astronomers agreed to call this unsavory place on the Moon the Lipsky Plain.

A landscape of about 100 craters, lying within a collapsed giant crater almost 500 kilometers (310 miles) across, was selected by the I.A.U. as a U.S. monument in honor of the American moon landing successes.

The giant crater is called Apollo. The small craters of the astronauts Anders, Borman, Chaffee, Grissom, Lovell, and White are together there in an intimate circle.

It's hard to believe that this sight will be omitted on your flight to the FSLO.

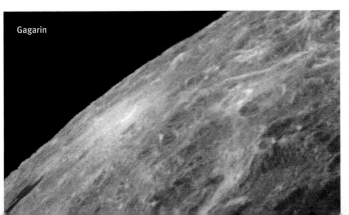

Gagarin

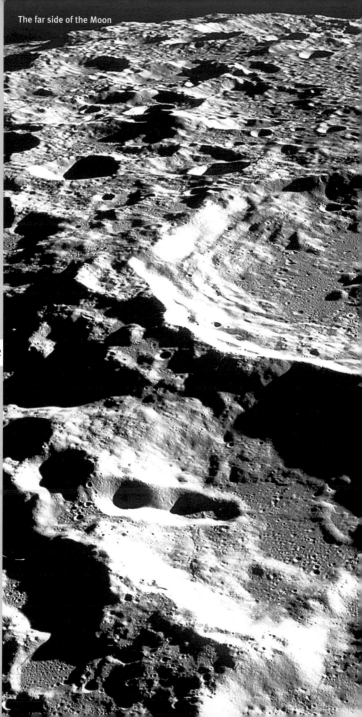

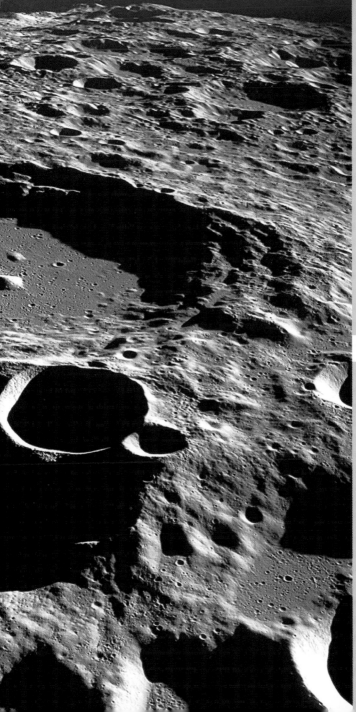

The Moscow Sea
Location: 25° N, 150° E
Sunrise four days after the last quarter

One of the few maria on the dark side of the Moon looks something like a figure eight. It was formed by a lava overflow from two craters that collapsed into each other.

This mare, more than 300 kilometers (186 miles) across, lies together with several craters that had not been flooded inside a still bigger crater whose wall has largely crumbled.

In the Moscow Sea there is an enormous single crater that was named for the cosmonaut Titow.

A large crater is dedicated to his colleague Vladimir Komarow. It borders on the Moscow Sea directly to the east. Komarow died on April 23, 1967, in the crash of *Soyuz 1*. As is now known, his space capsule tumbled helplessly during several orbits around Earth. When the drag chute opened, the ropes tangled, and the capsule fell to Earth like a stone. Komarow was the first victim of a manned space flight.

The Eastern Sea
Location: 20° S, 90° W
Sunrise three days before the full Moon

The Mare Orientale, 300 kilometers (186 miles) in diameter, lies on the border between the bright and dark sides, and thanks to libration up to half of it can sometimes be seen from Earth as a totally flattened surface.

You will see the beauty of this largest and presumably youngest crater as you fly over it. Two gigantic concentric circles, the outer one with a diameter of over 1,000 kilometers (620 miles), form the most impressive and most easily identifiable structure on the Moon's surface. From the surface of the Moon its walls form a formidable barrier.

The Trip Home

Departure Rituals

On December 14, 1972, Eugene Cernan spoke the official last words on the Moon: "I'm on the surface; and, as I take man's last step from the surface, back home for some time to come—but we believe not too long into the future—I'd like to just say what I believe history will record. That America's challenge of today has forged man's destiny of tomorrow. And, as we leave the Moon at Taurus-Littrow, we leave as we came and, God willing, as we shall return, with peace and hope for all mankind."

But when he had closed the hatch, Control Central clearly heard his last unofficial words: "Let's get this mother out of here!"

That's the way it will be for you, too: glorious feelings of gratitude, great emotion, and at the same time that good old reliable instinct of finally getting away from this hostile place.

As magnificent as your days on Earth's satellite may have been, you presumably would not have thrown a coin in the fountain even had there been one. None of the Apollo astronauts ever expressed a longing to go back to the Moon.

Now the joy of flying home has taken over, and the worst home-sickness you could ever imagine.

Takeoff from the Moon
Compared to the enormous expenditure of the liftoff from Earth, leaving the Moon is a prosaic affair. The lander lifts off rather shakily, but then accelerates powerfully and gets you to a speed of 5,400 kilometers per hour (3,348 miles per hour), until you are in moon orbit. There, weightlessness begins again, and the professional Apollo veterans urgently advise keeping your helmet visors closed. Moon dust and all sorts of other dirt that is unavoidable on a noncement liftoff pad, will be drifting through the lander.

> "Now I know why I'm here. Not for a closer look at the Moon, but to look back at our home, the Earth."
> *Alfred Worden* (Apollo 15)

Then comes the coupling maneuver with the moon space station, connected with the hope

that your LTV is really there ready for the trip home. The return firing is pretty long, but smooth and strongly accelerating.

Now you are looking at the Moon with new eyes when you see the yellow-black crater landscape. You will be happy to observe that the naked ball is rapidly getting smaller, and gradually Earth's gravity will be reaching out for you.

On the flight back, which like the flight out lasts for two and a half days, you'll feel like an old veteran in the cosmos. The actions on board are familiar, and astronauts report that over the course of time the cramped spaceship seems to get bigger.

Due to the stresses of the trip, the change in diet, and the effects of minimal or no gravity, you will have lost 1 to 3 kilograms (2.2 to 6.6 pounds) in weight.

> "We spent most of the way home discussing what color the Moon was."
> *Eugene Cernan* (Apollo 10, 17)

No cause for alarm, when you see Earth getting closer, if you only see a small crescent, for Earth, from space, looks much like the Moon. It has always astonished space travelers that Earth has the same phases as the Moon. We have in mind the image of the circular blue-white "full Earth," but in the reality of space this form is only to be seen for a relatively short while.

You are already familiar with the docking with the space station and transferring to the shuttle. But what now follows is another very risky part of your journey.

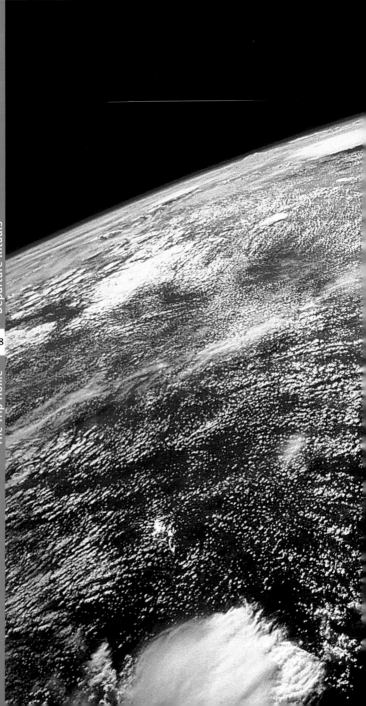

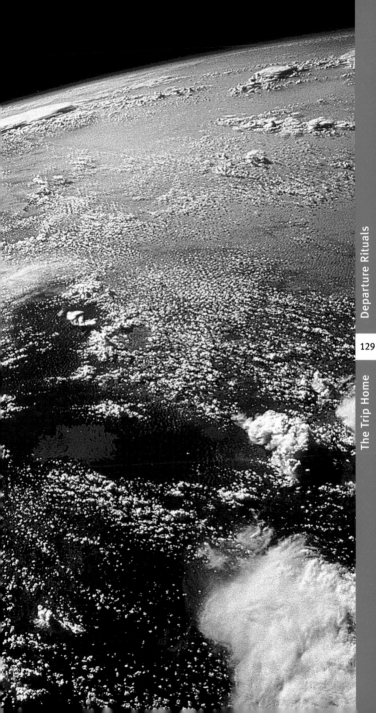

The Long Landing

Preparations

About six hours before landing you have to put on an antigravity suit, a kind of two-layer pants that can be inflated by means of a small air can.

During weightlessness, the natural blood-pressure compensation of your body stopped functioning. Once back on Earth, your blood vessels will not be able to adjust quickly enough. This would produce vein damage and considerable pain if you could not induce artificial pressure on your lower extremities with this special suit.

Then you get back into your contoured seat, buckle up, and wait for the jolt of braking ignition, which lasts for two and a half minutes. During this time there is transitory gravity in the shuttle, and you will be surprised by how many loose objects make their presence known.

Entry into the Atmosphere

One of the basic physical problems of every space flight is the reentry into Earth's atmosphere. A spaceship encounters the top layer of the air envelope at a speed of 28,800 kilometers per hour (17,856 miles per hour). The braking effect of the atmosphere creates such intense heat that every material, including stone and metal, would vaporize. At the same time, vaporization protects the spaceship itself.

This vaporization must proceed under the most precise control, before the entire heat shield is burned away.

To do this, the shuttle is kept at a shallow angle so that the heat stays within the range of 1,000°C (1,832°F) at the wings and 1,600°C (2,192°F) at the nose.

There is therefore a loss of material, and the heat shield of the space shuttle must be replaced after each landing. It consists of twenty-one thousand tiles of carbon-silicon foam, up to 10 centimeters (3.9 inches) thick. The tedious process of replacement is the major reason why space shuttles will never be able to be put into nonstop service.

The attachment of the tiles is critical. If even a few are damaged,

the heat of reentry would burn a hole in the shuttle, the oxygen would escape, and the temperature in the spaceship would become unbearable.

Something like this happened to the three cosmonauts on *Soyuz 11* on June 30, 1971: During a coupling maneuver in space, an oxygen valve was damaged, and in the heat of reentry the oxygen escaped faster than the life-support system could produce it. When the capsule landed on the Kazakh Steppe, the three passengers were dead.

Because of the intense heat, air molecules are ionized, and for about twenty-five minutes radio communication is impossible. For both ground control and pilots these anxious minutes are among the most unpleasant phase of the whole enterprise.

The Braking Phase

You will quickly be grateful for your antigravity suit, for during the braking phase your body weight will double.

Since as a passenger you were not trained in a centrifuge, you will face quite a challenge during the next ten minutes. Your face is twisted into a grimace and you'll feel how hard it is to speak and breathe. You will feel almost nothing of the tremendous temperature of the outer skin, but you will clearly hear the rushing and roaring of the air.

At a height of barely 100 kilometers (62 miles) the strongest braking ends; it's only half an hour to landing.

> "And when you come back there's a difference in that world now. There's a difference in that relationship between you and that planet and you and all those other forms of life on that planet, because you've had that kind of experience. It's a difference and it's so precious."
>
> *Russell Schweickart* (Apollo 9)

By now the atmosphere has reduced almost 95 percent of the previous incredibly fast momentum of the space vehicle. But you are still flying at a good 4,000 kilometers per hour (2,480 miles per hour) and are falling toward Earth at 50 meters per second (165 feet per second), with the air acting as a brake and the glowing outer skin slowly cooling.

At a height of 4,300 meters (14,190 feet) and a speed of 530 kilometers per hour (328.6 miles per hour), the actual landing approach begins. The pilots see the landing strip as a narrow line, which means that landing can only take place in perfect weather.

The Landing

The touchdown of a space shuttle looks far more elegant than the landings of earlier space capsules on water or on land. But next to liftoff it's the most dangerous part of your trip. In the landing phase the shuttle functions like a most peculiar glider.

Without engine power the 80-ton machine, steered by computer, glides down on relatively tiny wings on a steep path, and its landing speed of 300 kilometers per hour (186 miles per hour) would cause any glider pilot to panic.

The landing is a masterpiece of navigation: The braking procedure begins in the distances of space; course corrections are hardly possible in the reentry and heating phase, and then the runway, tiny in comparison to the depths of space, rushes up to meet you. Course corrections are even now only possible to a minor extent for the gliding giant.

For aerodynamic reasons, the landing gear can be lowered only at the last minute. Braking parachutes can't be used because of the shuttle's great weight, and the reverse thrust used by jets is impossible for gliders.

For these reasons, the shuttle needs an enormously long runway to land on. At present there are only four in the whole world: Cape Kennedy in Florida, a concrete strip at the Edwards Air Force Base in California, a salt strip 9 kilometers (5.58 miles) long in the Mojave Desert, and a runway at the Russian Cosmodrome in Baikonur. For emergency landings in Europe, the civilian airports in Cologne and Barcelona have been selected.

The shuttle-glider is very sensitive to side winds and runways wet by rain. This often causes shuttle landings to be diverted to another location or to be postponed for several hours.

So if your spaceship arrives happily back on Earth, you really have reason to celebrate. There is time for it, too, because before you disembark the highly poisonous fuel vapors have to be carefully pumped out. That takes about half an hour, and then at last you have reached the real goal of your journey: Earth.

The Florida Straits

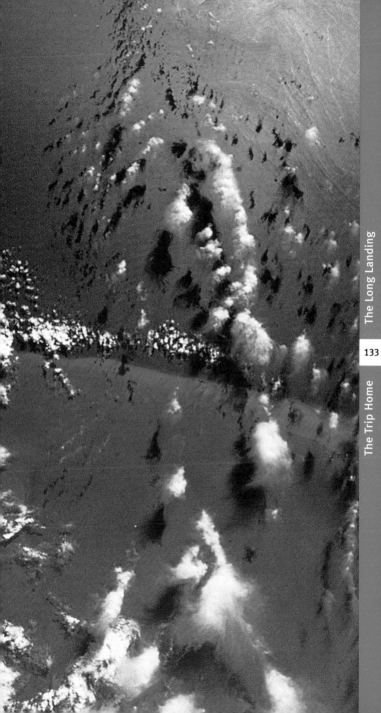

Back Home!

Leaving the shuttle, you will have to hold on tight when you smile into the cameras. Your legs aren't accustomed to gravity, and your circulation has gone haywire.

The shuttle is still radiating an enormous amount of heat, so be careful not to pass your hand over its skin in gratitude.

The first thing that awaits you is a thorough medical examination. You will have to go on wearing your antigravity suit for several days, and only after another thorough examination will you be able to resume your normal routine on Earth without aid.

You will have a lot to talk about. You will be questioned by relatives and journalists. At the same time, you will feel in a way like an interloper from a strange star. As after returning from a long stay abroad, you will be astonished at everyday things, and after your experience of extreme isolation you will need a lot of time for yourself. So don't plan anything strenuous for the week after the landing.

MOON TOURS
PRESS CONFERENCE

"Good luck, Mr. Gorsky!"

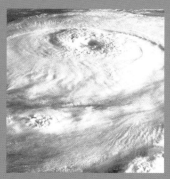

Resources

Recommended Reading

Maps

To prepare for your journey, you will need a proper atlas. The best one is Antonin Ruekl's, *Hamlyn Atlas of the Moon,* edited by T. W. Rackham (London: Paul Hamlyn Publishing, 1990). Developed in Prague, this atlas was made for earthly viewers, which means it illustrates the Moon's near side with all the distortion that is seen when viewing the Moon from Earth. It not only shows all the names of the craters and other landmarks, but gives a brief synopsis of the people they were named for. The book's appendix contains details on specific lunar places of interest, with beautiful photos shot by satellites.

The *Lunar Orbiter Photographic Atlas of the Moon,* a NASA publication (Washington, D.C.: U.S. Government Printing Office, 1971), is a nearly complete satellite atlas. Unfortunately, the book is out of print and can only be found in major libraries.

The most concise map available is *The Earth's Moon,* (Washington D.C.: National Geographic Society, 1976). At a scale of 1:10,000,000, it shows both the near and the far sides of the Moon on one sheet, together with an index of named formations and other lunar information.

Moon Globe

The only precise replica of the Moon we know of is made by the Columbus Company, D-72505 Krauchenwies, Germany, which can be found in some museum shops. It is equipped with a built-in light and shadow feature to simulate moon phases.

Reference Books

The ultimate collection of everything we know about the Moon's evolution and geology is *The Lunar Sourcebook* by G. H. Heiken, D. T. Vaniman, and B. M. French (New York: Cambridge University Press, 1991). In this seven hundred-page book, you will find much more than you will ever need to know about being a moon traveler.

The Once and Future Moon by Paul Spudis (Washington, D.C.: Smithsonian Institution Press, 1996) is a bit easier to read than *The Lunar Sourcebook,* and it contains exquisite details. In *The Once and Future Moon,* you can read

The Columbus Moon Globe

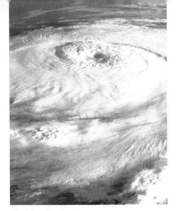

The Eye of a Hurricane

about lunar formations, evolution, and exploration. Especially helpful are Spudis's "four reasons to return to the Moon," which provides a thorough discussion of helium 3 and the proposed Far Side Lunar Observatory.

Facts and more facts are delivered by Kim Long in *The Moon Book* (Boulder, Co.: Johnson Books, 1995). *Moon Missions* by William F. Mellberg (Vergennes, Vt.: Plymouth Press, 1997) is a complete guide to all the Apollo missions.

Two books that contain "official" material are E. M. Cortwright's, *Apollo Expeditions to the Moon* (1975), and H. Masursky's *Apollo over the Moon: A View from Orbit* (1978). Both of these books were published by the U.S. Government Printing Office, but they are out of print and can only be found in major libraries.

The most recent tribute to the Apollo missions is Alan Bean's *Apollo* (Shelton, Vt.: Greenwich Workshop Press, 1998), a beautiful art book. The author was the fourth man on the Moon, and the

Apollo 12 experience shaped his life. After his return from the Moon, Bean, a gifted artist, made realistic and fictional oil paintings of the Moon.

Another artistic book about the Apollo expedition is for children: *The Sea of Tranquillity* (San Diego, Ca.: Harcourt Brace & Co., 1997) by Mark Hadden. This book is a carefully illustrated, lyrically written, and highly emotional account about July 1969, and how it affected a young boy's heart.

A Utopic Book

Carl Koppeschaar's *Moon Handbook* (Chico, Ca.: Moon Travel Handbooks, 1996) describes a trip to the Moon in a somewhat science-fiction-like manner. The book's foreword is written at Moon City in June 2020.

Films

Aside from the famous 1995 movie *Apollo 13,* featuring Tom Hanks, there is another classic worth seeing if you are considering a trip to the Moon: Stanley Kubrick's *2001: A Space Odyssey* (1968). This movie shows a journey to the Moon, with careful attention paid to the subtle details of space life such as weightlessness. The experienced moon guide reader, however, will notice some funny mistakes. During travel, the Moon changes its phases back and forth. Also, while the astronauts are in the Crater Tycho, Earth appears much too low on the horizon. Still, this movie is unsurpassed in capturing the exact look and feel of space travel.

Addresses

If you would like to contact former astronauts, NASA will forward your letters:

Astronaut Office / CB
NASA, Johnson Space Center
Houston, TX 77058

Some space travelers might also answer you directly if you enclose a self-addressed, stamped envelope:

Dr. Buzz Aldrin
Starcraft Enterprise
233 Emerald Bay
Laguna Beach, CA 92651

Neil A. Armstrong
P.O. Box 436
Lebanon, OH 45036

James A. Lovell
President, Lovell Communications
P.O. Box 49
Lake Forest, IL 60045

Dr. Sally K. Ride
Director, California Space Institute
University of California, San Diego
La Jolla, CA 92093

If you are interested in astronaut menus and would like, for instance, to arrange a future space party, you can turn to the producers of dehydrated space provisions:

Oregon Freeze Dry, Inc.
P.O. Box 1048334
Albany, OR 97321

Action Products, Inc.
344 Cypress Road
Ocala, FL 34472

The International Symposium for Space Tourism took place from September 5 through 7, 1996, in Bremen, Germany. You can obtain information from:

IP Space Tours GmbH
Hartmut Mueller
Postfach 1330
28847 Syke
Germany
Fax: 4242-38-91
E-mail: hartmut.mueller@emo.de

North Sea Coast

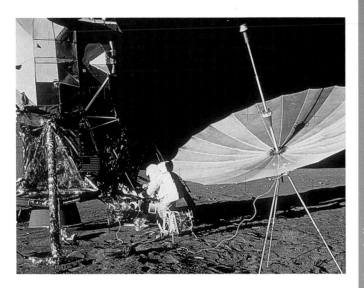

The Moon Online

If you would like to get an early and intensive introduction to the space scene, you will need a computer with Internet access. The amount of information available about space travel is enormous. Many publications no longer appear in print form, but only in electronic media.

Here is a small selection of Internet addresses. While surfing, take heed of the basic Internet premise and don't be surprised at anything.

http://spaceflight.nasa.gov/
The official NASA home page. From here you can spend hours surfing through the history, present, and future of American space travel. The FAQ section (Frequently Asked Questions) is especially delightful.

http://www.ksc.nasa.gov/
In case you want to access the Kennedy Space Center directly.

http://www.uah.edu/ASGC/academy
Current news about upcoming events at the NASA Space Academy in Huntsville.

http://cs005rm.iol.it/mirror/solar/moon.htm
One of numerous places to find detailed articles about all previous moon missions, for the most part reprinted with permission from the *Apollo Lunar Surface Journal*. Includes pictures from all missions. You can even download a few video films.

http://www.nrl.navy.mil/clementine/clib/

A first-class offering of the U.S. Navy. With the "Clementine Lunar Image Browser 1.5" you can, after entering the coordinates, look at superb photos from the Clementine probe. The Moon has never been so free and so complete.

http://www.magicnet.net/space.html
Here you will find a detailed presentation of the possibilities and risks of space tourism. Well, let's say more about the possibilities. Samuel M. Coniglio is a professional "Advisor on Space Tourism" and is happy for expressions of interest—without obligation, of course. From his pages you can reach with a click practically everything the Internet has to offer on space tourism.

http://www.buzzaldrin.com
The second man on the Moon has his own home page, a particularly offbeat one. Aldrin would like to boost space travel in a big way. High surprise factor.

http://www.asi.org
Twelve men have been on the Moon. When are you going? The Artemis Project will take you there! Very, very optimistic, but on hundreds of pages all the fine details about colonizing the Moon are discussed with great expertise.

http://www.museum.ru/Kosmonav/Exp1e.Htm
A tour through the Moscow Museum for Space Travel, with descriptions in tilted English ("Apparatuses in the sunny system").

http://www.west.de
A really fun address. Here you can win cosmonaut training in Russia's Star City and get extensive reports about the experiences of previous trainees. The exuberant pages are always good for a surprise. You used to be able to buy Russian cosmonaut suits, or at least a pair of gloves, but they are no longer being offered.

http://www.interglobal.org/isl/isl_home.html
A kind of space travel bureau is concealed behind this address. At least on the Internet, the era of Moon and Mars tourism has long been underway. Also accessible by mail:

Interglobal Space Lines, Inc.
P.O. Box 8947
Jackson, WY 83001
Tel.: 307-739-1296
Fax: 307-733-1391

http://www.incredible-adventures.com/
Another travel agent that offers specialties for space fans: Russian zero-gravity flights, training in various space camps, and far-out jet-fighter adventures. By mail:

Incredible Adventures, Inc.
6604 Midnight Pass Road
Sarasota, FL 34242

http://titania.osf.hq.nasa.gov/shuttle
In case you would like to turn your telescope on your future means of travel, a space shuttle flying by, or on the International Space Station (ISS)—here you will find liftoff schedules and exact flyover times for the individual continents.

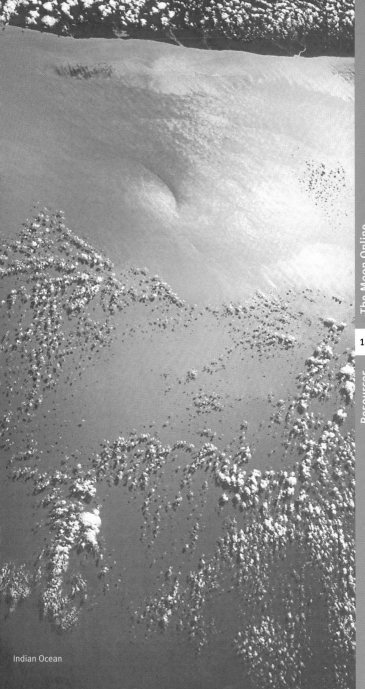

Indian Ocean

Index

Index